CRADLEY HEATH OLD HILL & DISTRICT

BRITAIN IN OLD PHOTOGRAPHS

CRADLEY HEATH OLD HILL & DISTRICT

RON MOSS & BOB CLARKE

SUTTON PUBLISHING LIMITED

Sutton Publishing Limited
Phoenix Mill · Thrupp · Stroud
Gloucestershire · GL5 2BU

First published 1998

Reprinted with corrections, 1999, 2002

Copyright © Ron Moss & Bob Clarke, 1998

British Library Cataloguing in Publication Data
A catalogue record for this book is available from the
British Library.

ISBN 0-7509-2066-1

Typeset in 10/12 Perpetua.
Typesetting and origination by
Sutton Publishing Limited.
Printed in Great Britain by
J.H. Haynes & Co. Ltd, Sparkford.

THE BLACK COUNTRY SOCIETY

This voluntary society, affiliated to the Civic Trust, was founded in 1967 as a reaction to the trend of the late 1950s and early 1960s to amalgamate everything into large units and in the Midlands to sweep away the area's industrial heritage in the process.

The general aim of the Society is to create interest in the past, present and future of the Black Country, and early on it campaigned for the establishment of an industrial museum. In 1975 the Black Country Living Museum was started by Dudley Borough Council on 26 acres of totally derelict land adjoining the grounds of Dudley Castle. This has developed into an award-winning museum which attracts over 250,000 visitors annually.

It was announced in August 1998 that having secured a lottery grant of nearly £3 million, the Museum Board will be able to authorize the start of work on a £4.5 million state-of-the-art interpretation centre. This will be known as the 'Rolfe Street Project', named after the street which once housed the Smethwick Baths. The façade of this Victorian building is to be incorporated into the new interpretation centre.

At the Black Country Living Museum there is a boat dock fully equipped to restore narrowboats of wood and iron and different vessels can be seen on the dock throughout the year. From behind the Bottle and Glass Inn visitors can travel on a canal boat into Dudley Canal Tunnel, a memorable journey to see spectacular limestone caverns and the fascinating Castle Mill Basin.

There are 2,500 members of the Black Country Society and all receive the quarterly magazine *The Blackcountryman*, of which 124 issues have been published since its founding in 1967. In the whole collection there are some 1,800 authoritative articles on all aspects of the Black Country by historians, teachers, researchers, students, subject experts and ordinary folk with an extraordinary story to tell. The whole constitutes a unique resource about the area and is a mine of information for students and researchers who frequently refer to it. Many schools and libraries are subscribers. Three thousand copies of the magazine are printed each quarter. It is non-commercial, and contributors do not receive payment for their articles.

PO Box 71 · Kingswinford · West Midlands DY6 9YN

CONTENTS

Corngreaves Furnace Company, successor to the New British Iron Company, *c.* 1901. Two of the blast furnaces beyond a large expanse of 'pig beds'. In the foreground pig iron bars have been loaded on to a railway truck. One can only admire the strength and stamina of the men: there isn't a crane in sight.

INTRODUCTION

For 160 years, since the rich seams of coal and iron catapulted Cradley Heath, Old Hill and their immediate surrounds into becoming the world centre of chain manufacture, the two towns somehow managed to keep their separate identities – though it was difficult to define their boundaries. As well as having the same industries – coal mining and chain making – they were part of the same local authority. From a Board of Guardians there followed the Urban District Council and then the Municipal Borough of Rowley Regis, which comprised five individual communities – Cradley Heath, Old Hill, Blackheath, Rowley Regis and Tividale.

Then someone in Whitehall became convinced that big would be beautiful. Despite a lively fight to remain independent, Rowley Regis (of Staffordshire) was forced to combine with Oldbury (of Worcestershire) and become Warley County Borough – a borough by name but, as many critics were later to say, one totally without character. A few years later Whitehall (and the government of the day) decided something even bigger would be even more beautiful, and thus the large and impersonal Metropolitan Borough of Sandwell, comprising towns like West Bromwich, Wednesbury and Smethwick, was created – in which the townships of the old Borough of Rowley Regis had nothing in common.

In later years the Royal Mail decided that their new computerised sorting system would operate more efficiently if Old Hill as a place name totally disappeared. Sure enough Old Hill was wiped off the bureaucratic map and became part of Cradley Heath; yet perversely Old Hill remains clearly marked on maps and road signs.

Of the two townships, Old Hill is by far the oldest. Although historical references to both towns prior to the mid-eighteenth century are hard to come by, there was a substantial settlement in Old Hill and the adjoining area of Reddal Hill. Cradley Heath on the other hand was precisely what the name suggested; it was a heathland of poor-quality soil on which a few squatters scratched a living and grazed livestock.

Close to the heath there was an area called Scolding Green, off what is now St Anne's (or Dudley Wood) Road. In the seventeenth century there was a cluster of cottages where some ironworking took place; some of the occupants also worked in the forge founded by Dud Dudley where the River Stour and Mousesweet Brook met, in an area still known as Cradley Forge.

By 1800 an iron industry had become well established together with a number of coal mines; the first entrepreneur was James Attwood who owned a large number of water-powered forges. With the advent of steam power he rapidly expanded his empire and from then on Cradley Heath and Old Hill mushroomed, as scores of large and small works (or chainshops) came into being. Hundreds of people migrated from the countryside attracted by higher wages, and dense pockets of housing were built alongside the works.

The photographs and drawings on the following pages recount the remarkable growth of a unique area. By the very nature of the area there was little that could be called photogenic, so very few people bothered with photography. As so often happens such pictorial memorabilia frequently gets destroyed in house clearances; the authors therefore count themselves fortunate that so many people have taken the time and trouble to seek out many old photographs that tell a story far more effectively than thousands of words.

CHAPTER ONE

AROUND THE TOWNS

Although the actual date of construction is not known, Corngreaves Hall was built by the eighteenth-century ironmaster James Attwood, and appears on an 1808 enclosure map. His son John sold the hall, estate and Corngreaves Works in 1826 to the British Iron Company, later to change its name to the New British Iron Company. The hall became the home of the company's manager. When that company was wound up its mines and hall were sold to the Garratt family. At the beginning of this century the hall was sold again, this time to Robert Fellows; his son later restored the hall and lived there until March 1950 by which time it had become widely known as Fellows's Hall. A member of the Fellows family told the authors that the Midland Red bus company offered the Fellows family around £60,000 for the hall and some of the land for use as a convalescent and rest home for its employees. The then Rowley Regis Borough Council got to hear of it and, in a special Saturday morning council meeting, agreed to place a compulsory purchase order on the estate; the amount paid was alleged to have been less than half the offer of the Midland Red. The council then built a vast housing estate – the Timbertree Estate – on the farmland and the former Timbertree colliery area. For a time some of the council's senior officers lived in the hall. Over the years the hall fell into disrepair but Black Country Society members successfully campaigned for the hall to be granted Grade II listed building status, thus forcing the current owners, Sandwell Metropolitan Borough Council, to begin restoration work; some of the restoration costs have been met by grants from the European Union.
But every cloud is said to have a silver lining. . . . Part of the hall's estate was incorporated into the adjoining Haden Hill Park to create a modest golf course.

Belle Vale, Cradley Heath, by the River Stour bridge which marked the county boundary between Staffordshire
Worcestershire, *c.* 1900. The two children are possibly with their nanny and could have come from Corngreaves Hall,
entrance gates to which are just out of view on the left. The chimney in the background belongs to Corngreaves Bri
Forge, a spade and shovel works mentioned in an 1893 sales catalogue. Its mill was powered by the fast-flowing Sto
The bridge was widened and strengthened many years ago but the older part still carries a tablet with the leg
'J.A. 1800' – probably referring to James Attwood, who lived at the hall and built the Corngreaves Works, late
become the New British Iron Company. In the background can be seen the waste mound of the New Hawne Colliery
the fuel crisis of 1947 much of the mound was removed; it contained thousands of tons of coal slack ideal for firing
boilers of Stourport Power Station. In 1974 the remainder of the mound was virtually levelled when what was left of
slack was taken to power stations as coal miners had gone on strike; the infamous three-day working week and widespr
power cuts followed.

en Hall, Old Hill, was the home for many years of the Haden family. The family line has been traced back to Walter
edene in 1270. Although the Tudor hall dates from about 1531 there is evidence, from the nature of construction of
ellars, that it replaced another large building.
his view of the south side shows the ancient sundial. The last direct-line Haden to live in the hall, Anne Eliza, died in
5. In subsequent ownership a Victorian house was built alongside the hall. The hall's landscaped parkland stretched
n the hill to the banks of the River Stour, bordered on one side by Hayseech and on the other by the Corngreaves Hall
e.
1922 the two houses and parkland were bought by public subscription for use as a public park, which included a
ber of pools and a large lake that once used to have its own boathouse. Shortly after taking over the park, the council
an open-air (and unheated!) swimming pool adjoining the former courtyard, stables and coach house.
he council, to its credit, carried out large-scale improvements and by the late 1940s Haden Hill Park was regarded as
of the best municipal parks in the country. During the early part of the war evacuee children from London were
ed in the hall for a time. Then in the 1950s the Victorian house was converted into a local museum under the
ction of the then borough librarian, J. Wilson Jones.
ter being partially gutted by fire in 1977, the hall lay in ruins for some time before a volunteer group successfully
paigned over several years for the Tudor hall's restoration, which is now taking place.

By the lack of people, trams and carts it can be assumed that this photograph of High Street, Cradley Heath, in ab
1920 was taken early on a Sunday morning. The dip in the road caused by the subsidence years before can clearly be se

High Street, Cradley Heath, c. 1909. The Royal Cinema was later built roughly where the two men are standing. On
opposite side of the road (extreme left) is Queen Street and, further down, King Street. To the right, opposite the h
and cart, is Bank Street which leads to Foxoak Street.

Halesowen Road, Old Hill, *c.* 1900. Many of the buildings in this picture still stand. To the immediate right is Trinity Street and the shop on the extreme right-hand edge of the photograph later became the offices of Gilbert Lee, a solicitor and clerk to the Rowley Regis magistrates. In the distance and before the parish church can be seen the bridge that carried the mineral railway from the New British Iron Company at Cradley Heath to collieries and the canal.

A rare though badly stained picture of Old Hill from the parish church tower, *c.* 1900. In the immediate foreground is Old Hill police station and magistrates' court. Behind those buildings is the embankment carrying the mineral railway between the Corngreaves Furnace Co. (successor to the New British Iron Company) and the collieries and canal near Powke Lane and Waterfall Lane. On the right can be seen the distinctive roof-line of the Trinity Schools. On the skyline to the left is the tower of Netherton parish church and (right) the Noah Hingley Ironworks at Netherton. Note that even in this urban and industrialised scene there were still some fields where cattle grazed.

Probably one of the best photographs ever taken of a typical Black Country local shop, this shows a shop in Waggon Street, Old Hill, one of the oldest parts of the district, 1928. The area was noted on an 1820 map as having densely packed houses, long before Old Hill had a town centre as such. This picture shows a young Joe Atkins sitting on his grandmother's lap while his Aunt Sophie is on the left. The reason for the shop-front decorations was Old Hill Carnival — as noted on the *Express & Star* contents bill on the wall. The houses stood in the shadow of the Waggon Colliery and were originally built for the miners. At the rear of the shop was a 'brew 'uss' (brew house) and chain shop, where the family could make a little extra money as chain 'outworkers' for one of the larger companies.

o contrasting pictures of the same area. Above: Halesowen Road, Old Hill, where the road divides to join (right)
uty Bank and (left) forms a crossroads with Barrs Road and Beauty Bank, c. 1900. The cottages shown disappeared
ny years ago and were eventually replaced by public gardens and benches. A single house was built at the rear of the
dens on Beauty Bank in the late 1920s. In the background can be seen the Birmingham–Stourbridge railway line
bankment, and beyond that is the outline of what was probably the Butterfly Brickworks. Below is a postcard view of
Barrs Road/Halesowen Road crossroads, c. 1958. To the left is one of the entrances to the former Rowley Regis
ough Council Offices – most irreverently referred to by locals, and the occasional bus conductor, as 'The Kremlin'!
d Hill Stationers)

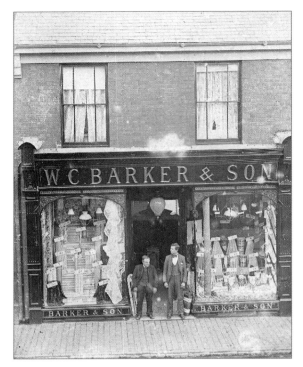

Left: W.C. Barker & Son's drapery and haberdashery shop in High Street, Cradley Heath, c. 1900. It was one of three branches, the other two being at Netherton and Great Bridge. The founder appeared to have considerable business acumen with wider interests than drapery; in an 1844 cash book are details of property and other dealings which netted him hundreds of pounds a time – at today's values we would be talking in scores if not hundreds of thousands of pounds. The shop was later bought by Mr E. Bowen-Davies who extended it to occupy what had been ground floor living accommodation. Below: the shop frontage, 1980s. After Mr Clive Bowen-Davies retired and sold the property, it later became an Indian restaurant.

for the cart wheel and other industrial debris, this scene in Halesowen Road in about 1920 could have been typical of
non-industrialised town. The bank on the left is a colliery spoil mound comprised mainly of marl, which in wet
ther turned into a grey sticky mass. This was cleared to make way for council housing and sheltered accommodation
the elderly.

ded picture of the Parsons family's sweet, confectionery and shoe shop in High Street, Cradley Heath. It was next
r (on the left) to Case's hardware and ironmonger's store. Mrs Parsons is standing in the doorway.

A well-known High Street, Cradley Heath, business for generations was that of H. Case, 'Wholesale Ironmongers Builders Factors'. In this detailed picture of about 1920 are seen wooden woven 'swills' (baskets) in which chainmakers used to carry breeze to the hearths. The right-hand side of the shop also specialised in household equipme while the left-hand side appears to have been the showroom. In later years the entry in the centre was rebuilt to form entrance to the shop. It closed in the 1990s – and with it went another bit of old Cradley Heath.

The Station Hotel at the Junction of Chester Road and Lower High Street (Lomey Town), Cradley Heath, c. 1900. The ho provided accommodation for artistes appearing at the Empire Theatre, High Street, as well as businessmen visiting the tov When buses put in an appearance all the Dudley services started from the railway station entrance on the extreme right.

Five Ways, Cradley Heath, 1920. Cartwright's clothing and pawnbroker's business stood on the corner of High Street and Graingers Lane. In the 1930s the property pictured was demolished to make way for the almost art-deco design of the Burton's store. Cartwright's moved to 44–5 High Street, adjoining the entrance to the market, where it remained until 1957 when it closed at the end of its lease. Pictured in the doorway is Mr Sydney Homer who managed the business from 1919, when he was demobilised after the First World War, until 1957 – a total of thirty-eight years, which must have made him one of the best known of the High Street traders. He and Mrs Homer then lived in retirement in The Crescent, Old Hill.

Before the arrival of the Merry Hill Centre and the clearance of many of the older housing areas of Cradley Heath, the High Street remained a busy place as this 1967 photograph shows. Yet apart from more modern shop-fronts, the upper storeys of most of the buildings had remained unaltered for nearly 100 years. The butcher's shop of Dennis Eyre was earlier owned by 'Jimmy' Dunn, who also had a shop in Netherton.

Cradley Heath, despite its youth when compared with other Black Country towns, soon gained a reputation of having the best market, with food and clothing usually cheaper than anywhere else in the area. Markets were held in the High Street until 1922. In that year 'Beggars Row' Market opened, followed not long afterwards by the Central (also known as Biggs's) Market. This picture, taken in 1967 shortly before the market closed so the site could be redeveloped, will bring back many memories for the older generation. The empty shop to the right was formerly owned by Mr and Mrs Read who specialised in fine bone china and figurines. On the left, there on a temporary basis, was the West Midlands Gas showroom; the premises had previously been occupied by one of the High Street's best-known businesses, Cartwright's (clothiers and pawnbrokers), who had moved there in the 1930s after having to leave their Five Ways premises – because of redevelopment by Burton's.

The entrance into the market (once known as Lloyds Market), looking towards its High Street entrance only weeks before it closed, 1967. The area was originally known as 'Beggars Row' – a reference to a row of extremely basic cottages built there in the mid- to late nineteenth century.

...is photograph was probably the last one ever taken in the old market hall. Its successor (on the same site) has never ...naged to capture the appeal of the old market – even if it has fewer draughts!

...ll known to many Cradley Heath and Old Hill people as Spinners End, this section of Upper High Street has undergone ...nsiderable change since this photograph was taken in 1973. While the properties on the left – such as Jones's shoe shop ...unded in 1875) – have changed little, a considerable amount of property on the right has been removed and a grassed ...a put in its place. This clearance was planned in advance of a proposed Cradley Heath bypass. Today, twenty-five years ..., the bypass is still being talked about in council offices.

There is nothing left of the houses seen in these two photographs of Graingers Lane, Cradley Heath. Above: a view from the direction of Five Ways, late 1960s. The shop to the right was once a grocery and sweet shop and then became a shoe repairers. Beyond the bridge, the white-fronted buildings facing the camera are Garratt's offices, thought to be among the oldest commercial buildings still standing in the town. Below: looking towards the town centre. On the extreme right is the slag wall (made up of waste from the former New British Iron Works), beyond which was a motor coach garage operated by the Newton family whose house adjoined the garage. Mr Bert Newton was one of the first 'horse-brake' operators to turn to the new-fangled charabancs in about 1920. The car on the left is parked outside the saddlery and leather goods shop of the Cole family. Both father and son worked on horse tackle, collars and saddles, as well as school satchels and bags, with the business dating back to pre-motor vehicle time. An activity Mr Cole junior was well known for was the restringing of tennis and badminton racquets.

would never have happened today! This group of cottages, believed to be of Tudor origin, stood in Hayseech, Old Hill,
a cart track leading from Hayseech Road. They were demolished early in the twentieth century and the site was left
elict until, in recent years, the area was redeveloped. The centre cottage was the home of a well-known Hayseech
nily, the Priests. This family picture of about 1900 shows (from the right) Doris Priest, Lucy Priest, Robert Edward
est (holding his daughter Gladys), Lawford Priest (who, after serving in the First World War, was a well-known local
nist and organist in Hayseech Methodist church), Alex Priest and a neighbour, believed to be Mrs Johnson.

new use for old houses. In an area adjoining Old Hill Cross there was a labyrinth of small streets and tightly packed late
ctorian and Edwardian terraced houses. Not without considerable local opposition, Warley County Borough Council
clared them unfit for habitation; it then invited its fire brigade to assist in the clearance by setting fire to houses and
en practising fire-fighting techniques in the early 1970s. The corner shop, far left, is still in business.

The changing face of Old Hill. Above: Wrights Lane, with the old New British Iron Works railway bridge abutment 1967. When the area was being cleared (despite the well-maintained houses) the embankment was removed and a JC attempted to break up the brickwork – but very nearly broke itself in the attempt! Eventually explosives had to be used so solid was the brickwork. Below: the same location only eight years later.

e last rag and bone man to operate in Old Hill with a horse and cart – Mr Roberts of Dudley, 1970. He was collecting
ap metal in Dudley Street and was accompanied by his two children.

ce a common sight but one which would send today's environmental health officers into a frenzy – a ton of coal being
vered in traditional manner; tipped into the road and on to the pavement at Dudley Street, Old Hill. The householder,
ess he wanted to pay someone else to do it, then shovelled the coal into the cellar (coal 'ole) through a removable
:ing or trapdoor, either on the pavement or in the house wall.

A well-known Old Hill business was that of 'Tommy' Patrick's butcher's shop in High Street with its immaculate sho
front and house next door. In the 1970s the slaughterhouse at the rear of the shop was carefully recorded, dismantled a
taken to the Black Country Musuem at Dudley for possible reconstruction.

Looking down High Street (now Highgate Street), Old Hill, from Garratts Lane. The bridge carried the Dudley–Old H
branch line with High Street Halt next to the bridge (left). Apart from the Fox Hunt public house, all the property s
on the left, including the British Oak (on the corner), the Queen and Bladen's sweet shop, was demolished in 1971.

original Rose and Crown in Halesowen Road, Old Hill, *c.* 1900. Many years later it was demolished and a new pub
he same name was built. It stands opposite the entrance to Haden Hill Park, although when this photograph was taken
park, its Tudor mansion and Victorian house were privately owned. The name of the licensee was Edge and it is
eved that his son Stanley, who was born there, was the design draughtsman at the Austin motor works who played a
or part in the development of the first Austin 7 in 1922. The story is told that he helped Sir Herbert Austin design the
using the billiard table at Sir Herbert's Lickey Grange home as a drawing board! Behind the horse and rider is seen
chimney of Haden Hill No. 2 pit. This was known as the 'pretty pit' because it was surrounded by trees. The owners
Iaden Hall had decreed that a rope railway be installed to carry waste to another of the colliery sites (Waterfall Lane)
hey would not have their view spoiled by a pit mound: very much a case of 'NIMBY' (not in my back yard)!

Cradley Heath and Old Hill, it is said, had more pubs per head of population than any other Black Country town – though local historians in Dudley and Tipton may dispute that claim. None the less there were a huge number of pubs and they owed their popularity to the large number of chain- and iron-working firms where men (and women) working by the furnaces for many hours regularly sent boys out for jugs of ale to quench their thirsts. One such pub was the Chainmakers' Arms, Corngreaves Road, Cradley Heath, which was known locally as the Chainees. Next door was the Queen's Head. Shortly after this picture was taken in 1970 both were demolished. A few years later all the old houses in Corngreaves Road had also been demolished, together with all but one of its six pubs.

Arguably the oldest licensed premises in Old Hill and Cradley Heath was Ye Olde Cross in Halesowen Road. It was one of the few buildings named in an 1820 parish map featuring Old Hill Cross. When renovation took place in the 1960s the roof joists were found to be little more than dressed tree trunks – though the exact age of construction has never been established. Next door (left) was the long-established chemists of Bellamy & Wakefield, opened in 1821 and closed 154 years later. The pub closed through lack of custom, but enjoyed a brief revival as Samuel's Night Club until being almost totally destroyed by fire. As this book went to press, the surprisingly unlisted building was demolished.

...e late 1960s wholesale demolition of hundreds of cottages and terraced houses in Cradley Heath and Old Hill – of the ... which today are in great demand – was underway. Such was the extent of the clearance that Warley County Borough ...ncil (successors to Rowley Regis Borough Council) and later Sandwell Metropolitan Borough Council were accused by ...y local residents and traders of destroying the area's character by 'ripping its heart out'. This was the scene in Cherry ...hard, Old Hill, in 1967 when the Cherry Orchard was only three years away from demolition. The dark stains on the ... were chimney flues from the house next door. The housing which disappeared was occupied for over 100 years by ...kers in local collieries, chain, nail, iron and brickworks. A large housing estate was eventually built in the area.

...g since gone: the King's Head in Elbow Street, Old Hill, which closed through lack of custom in 1972. A subsequent ...lication for the reinstatement of the licence was refused by the Compensation Committee, who said there were still ...en pubs within a quarter mile radius. The pub was said to have been over 100 years old.

One of the oldest pubs in Old Hill was the Rose & Crown, Reddal Hill Road. The cottage with its dormer window probably the oldest part of the building, the double-fronted section being built in about 1850 and the rest added in ab 1900. At one time it had its own brewery and also an exceptionally fine bowling green.

The Peartree Inn in Cherry Orchard, Old Hill, became famous over a wide area when it was featured in a documentary film, *Joe, The Chainmaker*. For the film a 'concert' was held in which the legendary Joe Mallen sang chainmaker bent a poker (and broke it!) between his teeth and a Special Constable on his rounds was filmed peer through the window to see 'what's goin' on 'ere then'. But fame did not save the pub. 'Freddy's', as it was affectional known, was bulldozed in the name of progress in 1968.

ther popular pub in its day was the White Swan in Halesowen Road, Old Hill. At one time, because it was almost
osite the local magistrates court, the decisions of the magistrates on the Wednesday morning courts were brought into
stion during lunchtime debates at the bar! The site now forms part of the car park for a building society.

Royal Exchange, Old Hill, stood on the corner of High Street and Halesowen Road, next door to the Sunday School
and St James's Methodist church – more popularly known as the 'rhubarb chapel'. By September 1987 the whole area
flattened to make way for a traffic island and a bypass for Old Hill.

Over 100 years old, the former Beehive with its imposing frontage to High Street, Old Hill, eventually became an off-licence and wine merchants, later owned by Mr Joe Slater. Subsequently it was taken over by Fosters. The doorway to the left of the building was the entrance to a small office where local council rates could be paid.

A pub that has survived the test of time even though all the houses around had been pulled down is the Swan Inn at the junction of Foxoak Street and Providence Street, Cradley Heath. Wholesale demolition of local housing in the 1970s left it in isolated splendour . . . but still (1998) it soldiers on, being particularly popular for its bar meals. At one time it was better known to the locals as 'Jasper's'.

A much larger than average public house for the area it served (and still does) is the Blue Ball on the corner of Peartree Lane and Petford Street, Old Hill. The reason for its size was its nearness to the large factory and drop stamping complex of Burton & Delingpole as well as a large housing area, among which were a considerable number of outworkers' chain, nail and metal oddwork shops — all of which flourished through from the Victorian era to quite modern times.

Many are the evenings when courting couples have taken to their heels
Haden Hill Park when this bell began 'to toll the knell of parting day'.
For many years Haden Hill Park was completely fenced in; there were
five entrances, and half an hour before they were locked the duty park
keeper used to ring the bell several times before beginning his lock-up
duties. The practice ceased when vandalism to the fencing made the
locking-up ritual an academic exercise.

Not long after Haden Hill Park was given to the local borough council, an effort was launched to found a Sons of Rest pavi
in the park grounds. It was built on the hillside overlooking rose gardens, the bandstand and the ornamental lake. This pict
shows the opening ceremony in October 1937, which was performed by the Mayor of Rowley Regis, Alderman Tho
Deeley (centre). To his right is the main benefactor, Cradley Heath industrialist Alf Ryland. To Ald. Deeley's left is the R
Walter C. Chrimes who officiated at the dedication service. To his left is Henry Woodhouse, followed by the well-known fig
of W.H. 'Billy' Mitchell, the local reporter for the *Express & Star* with whom he served for forty-six years and also a str
supporter of the Sons of Rest. Some years later he and some other local people founded the Cradley Heath Darby & Joan Cl

CHAINMAKING

The Mushroom Green area on the outskirts of Cradley Heath has become something of a time capsule of the earliest days of chainmaking in the district. Although the Black Country Museum has recreated a chainmaking shop as part of its attractions, Mushroom Green is unique. The chainshop and many of the cottages are as they would have appeared over 100 years ago and 'live' demonstrations of the hand-making of chain are regularly given. One of the most prominent families in the district was the Kendricks, who were engaged in the trade until 1965. Their chainshop and brewhouse now form the centre of probably the most important aspects of Cradley Heath's small chainmaking heritage. In this photograph of about 1905 the Kendricks pose for a family portrait outside their home: they are, left to right, Joe Poole (son-in-law), William Kendrick (founder of the firm), Harry Kendrick (the last owner who continued to make chain until his death in 1965 aged eighty), Ellen Kendrick, Ada Poole (née Kendrick), Carrie Kendrick and Lily Kendrick. The two children are Dora and William Poole.

The ironworking that was taking place during the seventeenth century and before occurred on the banks of the River Stour; its fast-flowing water provided abundant power for what, by today's standards, was a modest industry. But in those days the work carried out in the area was the cutting edge of new technology, which took a giant step forward when Dud Dudley took over his father's (Earl of Dudley) ironworks at Cradley, where the River Stour and Mousesweet Brook meet in an area known to this day as Cradley Forge.

Following the invention of 'grooved rolls' by Henry Cort in 1783, Cradley Forge began to supply 'round iron' to the area's growing chainmaking industry. Before this, the earlier ironworks provided wrought iron for Cradley Slitting Mill at Saltbrook to be prepared and supplied to local nailers – hundreds of men, women and even children who sweated away for little reward. When machines began to make nails in Birmingham the 'hand nailers' could not compete, but quickly adapted their hearths to join the already growing number of chainworks and back yard 'shops'.

Thus Cradley Heath and Old Hill took the first steps to becoming, quite literally, the centre of the British Isles chainmaking industry. So large did it become that its own trade union, the Chainmakers and Strikers' Association, chose Cradley Heath as its national headquarters.

There were many famous names associated with the trade, one of whom, Noah Hingley, moved from Cradley Heath to Netherton where he built a large canalside works, and became the district's first maker of cable chain, which he supplied to a Liverpool shipping line.

Although chain was the staple product of the area, which soon held a monopoly of chain supplied to the Royal Navy, many firms started to diversify and began to produce vast amounts of ships' tackle for Britain's merchant navy and fishing fleets.

In 1928 Mr Percy Jump, a director of Noah Hingley's, said during a meeting of the Staffordshire Iron and Steel Institute that there were 6,000 people employed in the chain trade in the district, producing 90 per cent of the chain manufactured in the British Isles.

In the nineteenth century, when the 'new world' industries of the USA began to expand – and wages in the Black Country remained pitifully low – thousands of people from the region and hundreds involved in the chainmaking industry of Cradley Heath and Old Hill emigrated to America's East Coast, particularly Pennsylvania, where vast resources of coal, iron and other mineral wealth were being exploited.

A century later many of those families, though divided by the Atlantic Ocean, have kept in touch; where families lost touch there are many Americans (together with Canadians, South Africans, Australians and New Zealanders) who are now returning to the area to try and discover their 'roots'.

Here, then, is a pictorial look at an area that in its day was a world centre of excellence.

iew of the Kendrick family chainshop and home, *c.* 1920.
te the iron tie bars running round the house to protect it
n mining subsidence. Underneath the house was a
ery of the Earl of Dudley's No. 25 pit which had worked
the 'thick' – a 30 ft thick seam of coal which, it is
gested, gave rise to the name 'Black Country' in the
eteenth century.

Mushroom Green chainshop before restoration, 1971. The wooden lean-to housed the electric blower which created 'blast' for the six hearths inside the workshop.

Above: the quaintly named Cottage of Content public house is on the right of this picture taken in Mushroom Green by Thomas Wallin with a modest Box Brownie camera, 1920s. The chainshop in the background has long since gone but the Narrow House and the pub building still remain. *Left*: Florence Wallin making small 'coil chain' in the chain shop on the right of the narrow house (above). These two pictures are believed to be the only ones still in existence of the area when was a hive of industry.

ranch of the Earl of Dudley's own railway network – which pre-dated the GWR in the area – was laid through
shroom Green in 1852. In this photograph of about 1920 several chainworkers' cottages and workshops can be seen.
rail network connected the Earl's Round Oak iron and steel works with his colliery empire and a coal wharf on the
fordshire & Worcestershire Canal at Ashwood. Branches were also built to serve sidings where coal was sold to local
chants, as well as direct supplies to local factories such as Penn's Ironworks in Cradley Heath. When the GWR built
ine from Stourbridge a branch was laid into the Cradley Heath goods yard. The Mushroom Green line was lifted in
2 and the track bed has become a popular walking area.

e face of a craftsman: Harry Kendrick, aged sixty-three,
king chain, 1948.

High Street, Cradley Heath, packed solid with women chainmakers and their supporters during the 'lock-out' of 1910 when the women struck for a 2½d per hour minimum wage. The woman in the centre standing on a cart and waving to the crowd is either Margaret MacArthur or Gertrude Tuckwell: they were both leading campaigners for women's rights. The lady in question is probably about to leave the gathering to return to London by train from Cradley Heath. This occasion could have followed a strikers' meeting in the Empire Theatre.

Women chainmakers, some with children in their arms, leaving a mass meeting – thought to have been in connection with the infamous 1910 lock-out, which took place after their claim for a minimum hourly wage was rejected by employers and they went on strike. The corrugated-iron building in the background could be an emergency exit from the Empire Theatre, Cradley Heath, where protest meetings were held. A few men also appear to have attended the meeting.

The national *Reynolds Newspaper* joined in the rumpus over the lock-out of the striking women chainmakers with this provocative cartoon that featured the former Negro slave Booker Washington, who rose to fame as an author. He was visiting this country at the time of the strike, when other newspapers were accusing the iron and chain masters of sweated labour and slave labour. The caption quotes him as saying: 'Ah, I can sympathise with those poor brave women – I WAS ONCE A SLAVE MYSELF.'

Lucy Woodhall was probably the last woman chainmaker to hand forge chain in the country. She started to make chain in 1913, when she was thirteen, and finally retired after sixty years in the trade having worked for a number of firms in the Cradley Heath area. She is seen here, three months away from retirement, making chain at Samuel Woodhouse & Sons Ltd, Corngreaves Road, Cradley Heath in September 1973.

Lower High Street at around the time the bulldozers were moving in to change the face of the town – and some locals s the town's whole character, 1970. Happily the Workers' Institute building today appears virtually unchanged from wh it was built with money left over from the public donations made in support of the women chainmakers' strike of 1910. is probably the single most important building remaining that is related to the town's chainmaking history. It was built 1911–12 and opened by the Countess of Dudley on 10 June 1912. Originally intended to be a centre of education f workers, it was also used as an early cinema, had a billiards and snooker room and, on the top floor, the 'Edna Hom Dancing Academy'.

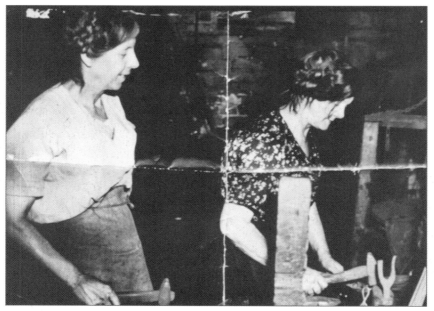

Chainmaking, of course, was the predominant industry in Cradley Heath and Old Hill for over a century, and even with the coming of electrically welded chain a surprisingly large number of customers had a stated preference for hand-forged rather than machine-made links. At one time it was hard to find a street in either of the towns which did not have at least one chainworks or a number of houses with 'back yard' hearths where women chainmakers shared the duties of housekeeping and motherhood with spells at the hearths as outworkers for larger companies. One such location was Plant Street, Old Hill, where there was a group of nine chain shops each with four or five hearths. Two of them formed the beginnings of B. & G. Williams, a company which is still operating today. Pictured are Mrs Woodhall (left) and Mrs Harriet Watts (right), making 'twisted' agricultural chain.

A typical women's chainshop in Cradley Heath, *c.* 1900. Before electric fans, 'blast' for the hearths came from hand-pumped bellows: the lady on the right is holding the bellows handle. On the extreme left and right are two young children; it was quite commonplace for mothers to take them into the workshop before they were old enough to go to school.

Women chainmakers at Harry Stevens Ltd, Oak Street, Old Hill, *c.* 1910. Left to right: Mrs Lizzie Wiggins (née Edge), Ruth Burns (there were four women named Burns working there), 'Aggie' Edge and Lizzie Westwood. The details for this caption were provided by Lucy Woodhall, believed to have been the last woman chainmaker in the country.

Mrs Elizabeth Jennings pumping the bellows in her own brewhouse chainshop at the rear of her home in Hall Street, Old Hill, in 1953. She was seventy-four when this photograph was taken, having begun chainmaking when she was thirteen. Looking on with a cup of tea is her neighbour, Mrs Perry.

Inside the small chainworks of I. Tilley, Crown Works, Cradley Heath, at the junction of Newtown Lane and School Street. For the fairly large chain shown in this undated photograph a smith and two strikers were needed.

A group of chainmakers and other workers at Richard Sykes & Son, Cradley Heath, 1920s. The works were bounded by Station Street, Graingers Lane and the railway embankment. They were world famous for their chain and shackle products and supplied the Royal Navy from well before the First World War. The chainmakers are proudly showing some of their products, while in the right background can be seen cable chain of the sort used with ships' anchors. We are fortunate (via the family of the late Joseph Billingham) to have some names. Mr Harry Billingham is seen fourth from left in the back row. He was a Chainmakers' and Strikers' Union Secretary. Other known people are Ike Billingham, Joe's uncle (second from the left), possibly T. Watts, Harry Billingham, Samuel Danks of Cradley and (with his clay pipe!) Harry Head of Cradley. Front row, left to right: J. Attwood, Noah Homer, -?-, Albert Beasley.

A group photograph of the employees at the Henry Reece chainworks, Maple Tree Lane, Cradley, c. 1950. Henry Reece died in 1925 and the firm was taken over by his son Glen (extreme right). The firm closed in the late 1950s and the premises were demolished in 1960–1. The works were next to the Reece family home, which still stands in Colley Lane.

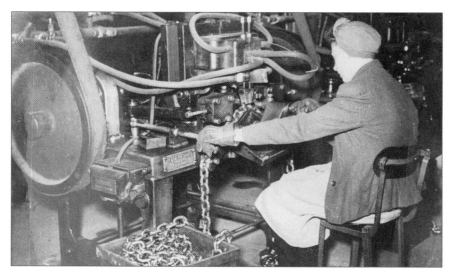

'It'll never catch on' must have been the words of many an old time chainmaker when he heard that electric welding of chain had been perfected. But catch on it did and here is a scene in a chain works. The development of the forming machine and the process of welding steel chain links was credited to a Monsieur Bosshard of France in 1901. The Cradley Heath firm of Samuel Woodhouse & Sons were the first chainmakers in the UK to use the machine and process in about 1901. The machine pictured was made by Holden & Hunt of Old Hill and these were in continual use from 1926 until after the Second World War. As part of the war reparations faced by Germany more modern chainmaking machines were imported into the Black Country.

Owing to the large amount of cable chain (such as that used for anchors) being produced in Cradley Heath, Lloyds built a second Test House – this time at Corngreaves Road, Cradley Heath. The last chain is thought to have been tested there in about 1960. The building is still in industrial use, though extra buildings and walled-up windows make a different picture today than when this photograph was taken early in the century. In the immediate foreground are the lines of the mineral railway from the Corngreaves Works. The pit spoil bank from the Bearmore Collieries can be seen to the left of the building.

CHAPTER THREE

THE DAY THE HIGH STREET COLLAPSED

Cradley Heath High Street before the subsidence, c. 1910. There was a comparatively level stretch of road from Five Ways (still known locally as 'The Ways') before it began to rise towards Four Ways in the distance. A postman looks quizzically at the photographer. On the extreme right is part of Cartwright's, clothiers and pawnbrokers.

The extensive coal mining under Cradley Heath and Dudley Wood – and to a lesser extent in Old Hill – led to subsidence which damaged property. Often the subsidence was of a gradual nature, but not so in Cradley Heath during the night of the 18th and morning of 19 February 1914, when about 200 yards of the High Street and its property dropped up to 3 ft in places.

According to newspaper reports of the time, during the evening and early hours of 18–19 February alarmed residents heard ominous creakings, as the walls of shops (all with living premises above) began cracking, and roofing timbers broke or worked loose.

People came out of their homes as one or two shop windows fell out, with bricks and roofing slates falling on to the pavements. At first light they were greeted with an horrendous sight. Contemporary reports say that the tram lines had lifted clear as the road surface dropped away from them, with pit gas seeping up from the collapsed workings and, as people stood and watched, the subsidence continued. Gas mains were shut off and, it was reported, smoking and all naked lights were banned.

The estimated cost of repairs to the road, services and property was put at 'around £25,000' – a huge bill in those days.

There was a searching inquiry into what and who was to blame for the subsidence. Eventually it was established that the Stour Colliery (off Graingers Lane and in an area known as 'Rattlechain') had been responsible. Apparently the old pit had been closed down some time before by its owner the Earl of Dudley, but a Mr David Parsons had leased the workings and reopened it.

Because of the thickness of the seam the practice was to leave a 39 sq. ft pillar of coal every 27 ft to support the roof, instead of using pit props. It was alleged that on reopening the pit the miners had been told to 'nibble away' at the pillars, with the result that first one and then others collapsed. Fortunately for the colliers the collapse happened at night when the galleries were empty, otherwise there could have been considerable loss of life underground. None of the local newspapers of the time – the *Advertiser*, *County Express* or the *Dudley Herald* – recorded any criminal or civil proceedings taken against Mr Parsons.

The following sequence of photographs gives some idea of the chaos that ensued.

This photograph was taken barely forty-eight hours after the subsidence had finally stabilised. Men work feverishly relay drainage and gas pipes while anxious property owners and shop workers talk in groups. A local policeman keep watchful eye on events. Several shop windows have boards nailed across them to support the frames. Centre right can seen the Talbot Hotel (also known as the Big Lamp on account of its lantern, seen here leaning at a marked angle over pavement). Today the dip in the road can still be seen; some people think that history may once again repeat itsel the water, which flooded the workings and became hydraulic with the pressure of the ground, ever drains away. . . .

Within hours of the subsidence traders and other business people – including solicitors – had formed themselves into the Property Owners Association to press demands for compensation from the colliery operator and/or the owner, the Earl of Dudley. Here a group of traders are lobbying shoppers and passers-by for support. The Maypole Dairy (right) was quick to assure customers it was 'business as usual'. Next door is Griffiths, jewellers and pawnbrokers, which also stayed open: in fact the family still run the shop in the same spot on which it was founded in 1899, and are looking forward to next year's centenary.

Some of the idea of the damage to property can be seen in this picture. While for Griffiths and the Maypole Dairy it is business as usual, the next two properties were not so lucky. They, like the Talbot Hotel opposite, took the full force of the subsidence; the entry has had to be shored up with timber, with huge cracks stretching to the eaves, and an equally severe crack in the wall has spread up and across the roof: the building appears to have broken its back.

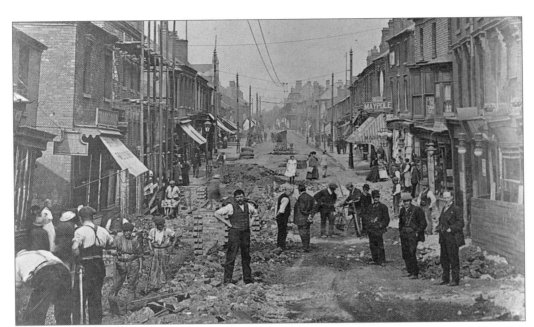

Repair work continues apace. On the left the stone sets which formed the road surface have been stacked up prior to relaying. On the extreme left is the lantern of the Talbot Hotel, with the building leaning outwards. On the opposite side of the road one shop front, minus its window, has been boarded up. In the middle distance what looks like a barrier has been erected to mark the safety limit for tramcars.

After the road surface had been repaired — although much work remained to be done on properties — High Street was opened to pedestrians. The local tramway company was quick to capitalise on Cradley Heath's misfortune and, it is said, ran extra services from Dudley and Blackheath for people to see the damage. Press reports at the time said thousands of people travelled by train, tram and horse brake to visit the town, and on the weekend of 23 February 1914 an estimated 30,000 visited the stricken town centre. This picture was taken that weekend.

CHAPTER FOUR

COAL MINING

A panoramic view from the Haden Hill No. 1 colliery (in the foreground) looking towards the Waterfall Lane pumping station operated by the Mines Drainage Commission – the tall building in front of a chimney in the centre, c. 1905. To the right, the low building with several hearth chimneys is Roland Barnsley's tube fitting works. He moved there from Newtown, Cradley Heath, where he had a gunbarrel works, the machinery for which was powered by the Mousesweet Brook: those works were recorded on the 1822 Ordnance Survey map.

Cradley Heath and Old Hill lie above the '30 ft thick', a seam of coal which in places comes quite close to the surface. Some historians say it was the ease of access for the primitive science of mining that gave the region its name of the Black Country. Another suggestion for the name is claimed to have come from Charles Dickens, who on a visit to Dudley looked down towards Netherton, Old Hill and Cradley Heath, and was so shocked by the pall of smoke hanging over the area that he was reported to have said: 'God help those poor people in that Black Country.' Needless to say, the debate about how the area got its name continues. . . .

It is fair to say that whereas forty years ago to admit living in the Black Country to someone from further afield was sure to bring looks of disdain, the opposite is now true. The coal mining legacy together with the ironworking and chainmaking that abounded has given rise to something of a boom in heritage tourism. Now, it appears, if you say you come from the Black Country you are looked at in a different light. A suggestion that apparently came from Sandwell Metropolitan Borough Council offices that it would be more politically correct to call the area the Grey Country has been greeted with howls of disbelief and derision.

Be all that as it may, the ease at which coal was mined meant almost a free-for-all as deep holes or primitive shafts were sunk throughout the area. The arrival of the canal through Old Hill in 1798 and, in the earlier part of the nineteenth century, the Corngreaves Iron Works, led to an even greater expansion of mining.

As the mines began to be worked out and were closed all that was left was vast spoil heaps, many of which survived into the 1950s. And there was (and still is) the legacy of subsidence; in 1967 a series of ground collapses pinpointed the existence of former workings which had never been recorded.

The 'landsale wharf' (where local merchants could buy their coal) at Haden Hill No. 1 colliery near Waterfall La c. 1890. The shaft for this pit was sunk by A.H. Barr & Co. in October 1834. This and the No. 2 pit (sunk in 1865) w bought by Walter Bassano of Old Hill in about 1865. The former Pig Lane, an ancient road from Haden Hill to Cradl may have been renamed Barrs Road after Mr A.H. Barr.

east sixty years separate these two pictures. Above: Haden Hill No. 1 Pit, *c.* 1900. The towpath goes over the bridge,
er which the canal split into two arms each with its own loading stages. On the towering pit mound can be seen
ke from coke ovens – the coke then being sold on to local chain and nailmaking shops. Coal was shipped out by
ow boat to many local canalside factories. To the right (and some years later) wharves were built to serve Lowe's
er yard, which for many years received the bulk of its timber by boat from Gloucester and the Trent, Mersey and
nes docks. Below: the same area, 1962. The pit bank (or 'bonk' in the local dialect) has been cleared and the canal
filled in. The canal has begun to silt and weed up, as the waterborne timber trade had ceased years before. All that
ains the same is the towpath bridge.

Haden Hill No. 1 Pit screen and 'land sale' wharf (where local coal merchants used to collect loads), just off Water Lane between Old Hill and Blackheath. A continuous ropeway hauled trucks carrying coal from the workings to screen and wharf as well as spoil for the pit bank, otherwise known as Barrs Bank: the pit owners, who lived near colliery, didn't wish to see a spoil heap from their back garden! But, 'tis said, the past comes back to haunt you – whic what happened to a hapless JCB driver whose machine fell into the tramway tunnels under the road during pipe la some fifty years on. With the passage of time everyone had forgotten about the tunnels – which can just be seen at foot of the slope in the older photograph.

en Hill No. 2 Colliery was sited almost opposite Haden Hill Park, then owned by the Haden family, who insisted that the ead was surrounded by trees and flower gardens and that spoil must be dumped elsewhere rather than harm their view. as not long before locals gave it the name of the 'pretty pit'. The first shaft was sunk in 1865, this picture was taken in at 1890 and the pit closed in about 1907. The land is now occupied by a Masonic hall; many of the trees still stand.

of the two canal arms serving the Haden Hill No. 1 Pit. Boat loading and unloading in those days was a manual job, each boat carrying about 30 tons. Note the electric lighting on the wharves. On a substantial amount of the ningham Canal Navigations twenty-four hour working was quite commonplace, such was the seemingly insatiable and for coal by factories and foundries. Note also the boat's tiller, known in boating terms as the 'ellum' (helm), h could be fitted at either end thus avoiding the arduous job of 'winding' (turning) the boat.

The breeze (small coke) or glede ovens on a pit mound, 'Barrs Bonk', off Waterfall Lane. These ovens turned small into small pieces of coke. Many tons were needed to supply the growing local chainmaking trade: the acrid black s from them added to the already heavy polluted air of this part of the Black Country and was another reason, perhaps, the Black Country got its name. The small brick building was the 'hovel' where the men who tended the ovens roun clock could rest, have their 'snap' (snack) and 'mek ther tay' (make their tea).

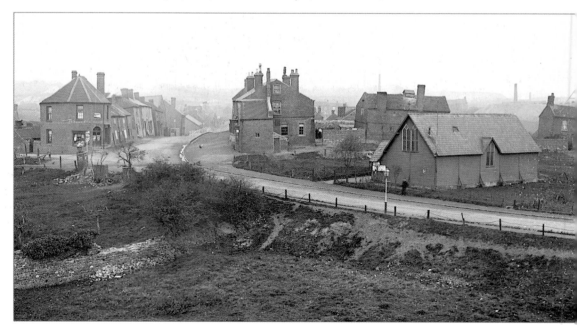

One of the best photographs ever taken of the effects of mining on a community (other than the chaos of the Cr Heath High Street subsidence) is this one of Dudley Wood Road, c. 1900, with a row of houses looking as if it is abo collapse backwards. On the right a house alongside the Earl of Dudley's railway line is leaning sideways.

CHAPTER FIVE

NEW BRITISH IRON COMPANY

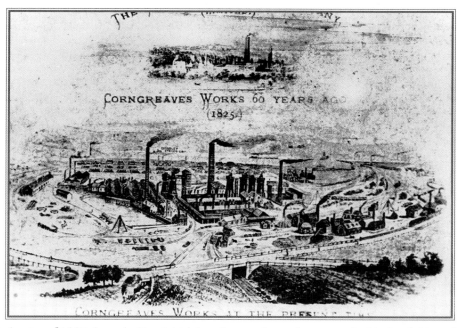

This drawing of 1885 shows the New British Iron Company's complex in considerable detail. Not only does it appear to have been drawn to celebrate the company's Diamond Jubilee in Cradley Heath but, as it turned out, it could well have been the company's first move to create a favourable public relations image prior to seeking a buyer; only a few years later the company went into liquidation. In the picture, bottom left, Belle Vale and Overend Road meet Corngreaves Road. The first bridge is where the works railway went to the Hawne Colliery, near Halesowen, while the other could be a line that served the Timbertree Colliery, believed to have been a rope-operated tramway. Corngreaves Road borders the works' site to the right; the other road must have been the original route of Pig Lane (Barrs Road). A line also came from the works, crossed Overend Road and ran to the Whitley Colliery between Cradley and Halesowen. In the centre of the picture are the blast furnaces, while to the left of them is the works pool.

Although the New British Iron Company Ltd of Corngreaves Works, Cradley Heath, and its successor were without doubt the biggest single employers in the town for at least eighty years, it was the Attwood family, then owners of Corngreaves Hall, who built the first ironworks at Corngreaves in 1810 – just at the time Cradley Heath was beginning to change rapidly from heathland occupied only by squatters and used as grazing for cattle and horses. By all accounts the land was of poor agricultural quality.

The Attwood family had been involved in iron working for 100 years before; their many mills on the banks of the River Stour were contained in a 1735 list of water power sites. One such forge was situated in front of the hall at Belle Vale (see page 10). The brickwork of the original forge can still be seen in the undergrowth.

With the expansion of iron and coal mining and the development of steam power James Attwood moved swiftly to further his fortunes, and moved on to land at Corngreaves. By 1825 the works and their associated collieries and brickworks interlinked by mineral railway lines (with links to the Dudley Canal and, later, the Great Western Railway) attracted the attention of the British Iron Company headed by the Duke of Sutherland. In that year the Attwoods sold out to the British Iron Company for the then huge sum of £600,000. The prospectus of the sale described the concern as 'comprising 208 acres containing collieries, claypits, brickworks and railways'.

On 2 November 1843 the company became known as the New British Iron Company. But by 1860 iron production in Cradley Heath had passed its peak. While chainmaking continued to expand, the local collieries and iron seams were being worked out, with the ironmaking industry being overtaken by competitors – not only in parts of the Black Country where richer seams of coal and iron were being exploited – but further afield, for example, in the north-east of England and South Wales.

The writing was on the wall, and by 1887 it had become known that the company was in difficulties. On 12 August 1899 it went into liquidation. Attempts were made to auction the company but there were no takers. Eventually production stopped, and the empire was split up.

Some of the blast furnaces came back into use, however, when they were bought by a consortium of local businessmen, one of whom was a Mr Alfred Bassano of Old Hill. They eventually closed down for good in 1912. But even as late as the mid-1950s memories of the once mighty blast furnaces lingered on as mounds of rubble until the whole area was cleared when the Porters Field Industrial Estate was developed. However, a few buildings bordering Corngreaves remain and are occupied by small engineering firms.

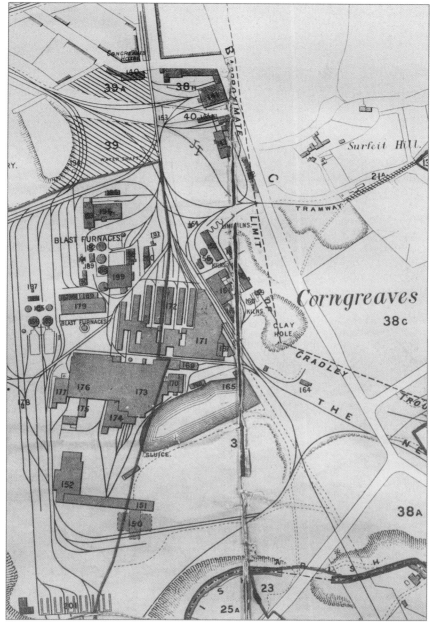

When the New British Iron Works was put up for auction by the receiver in 1893, this plan was published with the sales brochure. The company's own network of narrow gauge railway lines can be seen running out of the works in different directions. At the top of the map the line went part way up Corngreaves Road before swinging right to head for Old Hill, a number of collieries and the Dudley No. 2 Canal. Towards the bottom right, lines ran to New Hawne and Timbertree collieries, while in the centre right another tramway ran up Surfeit Hill to the 'drift' mine cut into the hillside, which is now covered by protected woodland at the top of Codsall Road. There are still remains of where this line ran; a gap between the boundary wall of the Bull Terrier public house and the pavement in Surfeit Hill marks the line's route. In the bottom right-hand corner a line crossed Overend Road en route to Whitley Colliery.

This view shows in considerable detail a large part of the Corngreaves works in 1885 and illustrates the accuracy of artist's work. This photograph was probably taken near one of the two bridges in the vicinity of Barrs Road. One of two lines to the left has a rope or cable attached to the trucks: this could have been operated from a colliery wind engine in a local colliery and on a steeper gradient than the locomotives could cope with. The works pool, possibly in earlier life a fire clay pit when the furnace linings were being made, can be seen in front of the works. The blast furna can be seen between the two chimney stacks. The railway trucks in the cutting were perhaps loaded before being taken the GWR sidings at the far side of the works land, as a wheel near the building in the foreground could have been par a mechanised tipping device for the colliery trucks.

The base of one of the two furnaces still operating, *c.* 1900. The men are lifting the pig iron bars from the sand beds (moulds) into which the molten metal had been run from the furnaces. There are members of Cradley Heath families who can remember their parents telling them that when the furnaces were 'tapped' during the night it was possible to read a newspaper in Graingers Lane. Note the railway engine in the background; it had no cab and could have been one of the original engines belonging to previous owners of the works.

When rope or cable was not used to haul trucks from the works to the collieries, narrow gauge steam engines were in constant use. Running on a 3 ft 2½ in gauge, they travelled considerable distances to collieries further afield and to the Dudley Canal wharves beyond Old Hill. *Mabel* was one of those locomotives; she was not, however, one of the engines from the former New British Iron Company owners, but was bought by the later owners, the Corngreaves Furnace Co., from W.G. Bagnall Ltd in 1899. Also in the picture (on the right) is stacked pig iron.

Another piece of New British Iron Company history was photographed in August 1976 just before the ground was cleared for redevelopment: beside the 'egg-ended' boiler is a large crank from a steam engine, which if in existence today would almost certainly have been preserved. One of the authors remembers as a child a number of skeletons of old traction engines, pipework and other boilers, which were a popular playground for children in the war years.

On the New British Iron Company site at the entrance from Corngreaves Road are the remains of this old weighbridge office, the date of which is unknown. At one time huge suspended gates on rollers could be drawn across the entrance to the site – and they were quickly dubbed 'The Golden Gates' by local people. The iron company's mineral railway from Old Hill and the canal entered from Corngreaves Road after passing alongside the Samuel Woodhouse & Sons chainworks and under the GWR bridge, which can just be seen in the background. The external appearance of the office was strongly reminiscent of the canal toll offices found in the Black Country.

CHAPTER SIX

TRADE & INDUSTRY

Mr Alan Walker at work in the back yard chainshop behind his home in Claremont Street, Old Hill, September 1973. When Mr Walker died his chainshop was offered to the Black Country Museum: it was dismantled brick by brick and reassembled there. It has the distinction of being the first building completed at the museum.

When Birmingham staked its claim in the nineteenth century to be the City of a Thousand Trades the Black Country was quick to respond by claiming to be the Workshop of the World. The latter phrase was later used at the height of the nation's manufacturing success to describe Britain on the world's stage.

For the best part of 150 years Cradley Heath and Old Hill retained their reliance on the iron-working tradition – whether it be chain, anchors, or ships' tackle. Brickmaking was another industry which flourished in the area, and that was something of a by-product of the mining industry; as pit shafts were sunk, often they cut through beds of clay. Some of this was ideal for building bricks while another type of clay, fire-clay, was suitable for building the lining of furnaces.

Eventually, partly because of the almost in-bred devotion to iron-working and partly because there was no room in which to expand into new industries, the district's traditional industrial importance began to fade.

Today there is still an iron- and metal-working industry; it is still possible to hear the crash of a forge hammer, the smell of a foundry or engineering works. However, on the site of former ironworks or coal waste mounds you will find large and small industrial sites and, as they were 170 years ago, small firms are starting up. Could this be the start of a new Black Country for the millennium? That may well be the subject of a book in 2098!

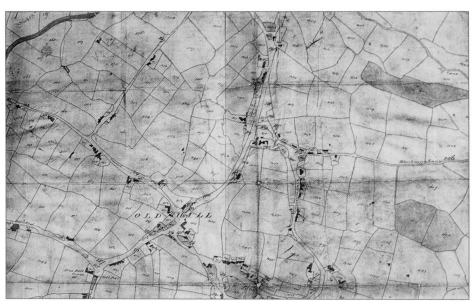

An interesting section of the Rowley Regis parish map, *c.* 1820. It shows, running from top to bottom, the Halesowen Turnpike Road. In the top right the road running to right centre is Pig Lane, later to be named Barrs Road. The road leaving the turnpike road and going right divides. The road that then runs to the right was Blakemore Lane; in later years the first portion became Peartree Road after which it became little more than a cart track running (as it still does) between Burton & Delingpole's works, through the railway embankment at Buck Tunnel, to emerge in Codsall Estate and Surfeit Hill, Cradley Heath. The other road is Lawrence Lane, which still follows its original line to Reddal Hill.

It is interesting to note that the only communities of any significance at the time were the area where Lawrence Lane left the Turnpike Road (Halesowen Road); what became Old Hill Cross (with Ye Olde Crosse clearly marked); and Reddal Hill. The first house in Reddal Hill was Reddal Hill House (built in 1759), which eventually became the Liberal Club. The First Charity School was built opposite in about 1790 and later rebuilt as Reddal Hill Schools.

Moving towards the lower left-hand corner is the junction of Halesowen Road and Cox's Lane, formerly known as 'Endless Orchard'. At that point there was a toll house and bar.

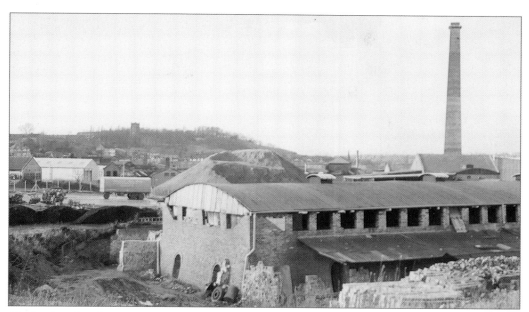

The brickyard at the extremity of the iron company's land from near the end of Pig Lane (Barrs Road), 1970. In the iron company's sale particulars of 1893 this was still officially named Pig Lane; it was believed the name was changed in the early 1900s when housing started to appear there and residents preferred another name! The brickworks, known locally as 'The Brickle', had a large Hoffman brick kiln, and the 'common bricks' it produced can be seen stacked alongside. One or two remnants of the company's large complex of buildings can still be seen in this photograph, including the large chimney-stack in the centre.

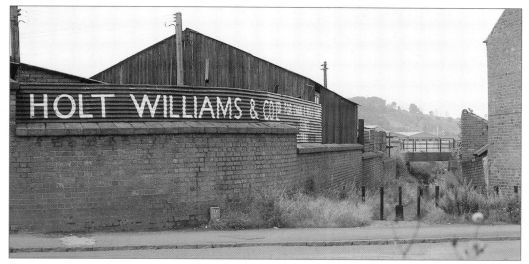

Near the junction of Graingers Lane and Corngreaves Road there remains this small spot of old Cradley Heath. The brick wall, well over 100 years old, marked one of the boundaries of the New British Iron Company, and when this picture was taken the factory above was of Holt Williams & Co., chainmakers. The cart track is still known locally as 'Rattlechain' on account of the noise of the chains used at the local colliery. The bridge (there used to be two) crossing the track was built by the Great Western Railway in about 1870 to provide sidings on the iron company's land. Beyond the track, once wasteland with ruins of part of the iron works, is now Porters Field Industrial Estate.

Once a common sight on the canals but now something of a curiosity or museum piece: an old 'spoon' dredger at work removing silt from the wharves at Noah Hingley's, Netherton, 1953. The boat was equipped with an enormous spoon which was manually operated to dig the silt out – an extremely arduous job for its crew. Although this waterside scene has long since disappeared, it is a fair bet that when this particular section of canal is drained for maintenance, a substantial amount of coal will also be found.

Until this Yelland photograph was discovered by the Black Country Society Industrial Archaeology Group members it was thought no photographs of the historic Cradley Forge had survived. Pictured at the turn of the century are the rolling mills, with the chimneys and Rastrick boilers of the wrought-iron plant in the background. The River Stour, which provided the power for the mill from when it was founded by Dud Dudley in 1610 (or possibly earlier) until steam power arrived, can be seen. The forge was closed in December 1906 and demolished in May 1907.

Noah Hingley (1796–1877) established his new iron works on the side of the Dudley No. 2 Canal at Netherton in 1837, his move prompted no doubt by the need for more room and the added attraction of a canal. His earlier premises were in Newtown, Cradley Heath. In this postcard of about 1905 boats can be seen being loaded and unloaded. Most were known as 'day boats' in that they were used locally between Mr Hingley's blast furnaces near Old Hill and brought pig iron to Netherton for puddling into wrought iron. The 'dampers' on top of the puddling furnace chimneys can be clearly seen. The bridge connected the main works with the Hingley chain works on the other side of the canal. On the extreme left stacked pig iron can be seen. The term pig iron came about because it was said the bars looked like piglets lying next to the sow!

This detailed photograph encompasses Waterfall Lane on the right, a large pool in the foreground, Dudley No. 2 C[...] running across the centre and Old Hill railway station with its triple junction. The pool was formed from a clay pit w[...] may have provided the puddling clay for the bed of the canal when it was built in 1798. The chimney was part of [...] pumping station built by Old Hill Drainage Company to prevent local mines from flooding. The water was dischar[...] into the pool and was eventually passed on to the canal. At the top left is a clear view of the railway junction, with [...] Halesowen line curving to the left, the Stourbridge line running to the top centre and the Windmill End and Du[...] branch line running parallel with Wrights Lane. The site of the pool and land bordering Waterfall Lane is now on[...] Sandwell Metropolitan Borough Council's (formerly Rowley Regis Borough Council's) depots.

Many and varied were the trades carried on in Cradley Heath, Old Hill and district a century ago. Birmingham called itself the City of a Thousand Trades; the Black Country was justified in calling itself 'the workshop of the world'. Although mining, ironworking, and brickmaking were the staple industries, there were also other important trades – such as the cooperage firm of Thomas T. Smith of Hollybush Street, Cradley Heath. Their barrels were in great demand as much of the smaller chain, ships' tackle and hardware was carried in them; equally there was a big demand from the dozens of breweries, large and small, which needed them. In this picture of about 1912 twelve-year-old Bertram Smith is seen on the cart, which is carrying wooden and metal hooped barrels and a chainmaker's box.

Another view of the Smith cooperage, c. 1905. In the yard entrance, later covered over, can be seen staves and hoops weathering. In the background are the roof and air vents of one of the many chainshops in the vicinity. The house was built in 1904 at a cost of £200. Pictured in the shop doorway is Elizabeth Smith, with Thomas Smith senior and Bertram Smith; the name of the man on the right is not known. The notice on the gatepost advertises Royal Daylight Lamp Oil (paraffin), and in the shop window can be seen almost every kind of paraffin lamp and container. The shop also sold firelighters. The firm moved in the 1970s to Porters Field Industrial Estate when Hollybush Street became part of a council clearance scheme; when it went into new ownership it was believed to be the last traditional cooperage left in England.

On 4 July 1906, while our American cousins were celebrating Independence Day, there was a huge explosion in Cra
Heath when a large boiler at the Providence Works of William Penn exploded, killing three people and dama
property over a wide area. Above: the utter devastation at the works shortly after the blast. In the foreground a
number of wrecked railway trucks belonging to the Earl of Dudley, which had brought coal from his collieries in
Pensnett and Sedgley areas, while the rubble centre left is all that remained of the boiler house. Below: the chainw
yard of Woodhouse Brothers, Newtown Lane, where a piece of the boiler, hurled over 150 yards, landed, narro
missing some workmen. Among those surveying the wreckage are Albert Woodhouse (extreme left) and C
Woodhouse (third from left).

…en the 30 ft long and 6 ft diameter boiler literally took off in …es through the roof of Penn's ironworks, the largest single … was hurled almost a quarter of a mile and crashed down …nd properties in the High Street. It is pictured here in the yard …ammersley's shop near Four Ways. In the explosion two men … factory were killed and ten were injured, some seriously, by …, scalding water and flying debris. The third death, that of a … in a nearby house, was caused by rubble crashing through the …g room window.

…distinctive office block of Clyde Works, Corngreaves Road, Cradley Heath, 1976 – prior to its demolition to make …or modern industrial units for the Folkes Group. Had it been standing today it could well have been protected by …l building status. The building stood opposite the former chain works and chain testing bed of the New British …works Company Corngreaves works.

The two boiler erection towers of the Cradley Boiler Company, 1980: they were demolished shortly afterwards. At the time they were thought to be the last such towers remaining in the country; the tower on the left was made of wood and was the oldest. Boilers were erected upright for ease of assembly and riveting. The company moved to Cradley Heath in 1875 from an earlier works at Cookley, near Kidderminster.

Inside Cradley Boiler Company, 1975. Most of the machinery was still using the belt-driven system from a central power supply. Although the company has now left this site it is still in operation, and recently installed a Cradley Package Boiler in the Bratch water pumping station, Wombourne, to enable the original steam engines, now being restored by steam enthusiast Len Crane and his team, to run again on open days for the benefit of tourists and industrial history groups.

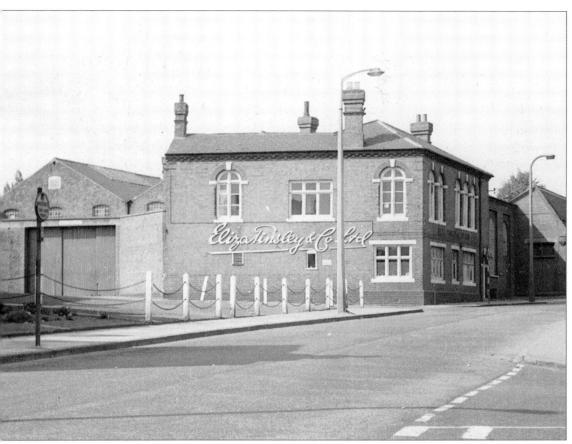

story of Eliza Tinsley & Co. Ltd of Old Hill is also the remarkable story of a woman, widowed at the age of thirty-n, who took over her late husband's company and built it up to be one of the largest concerns of its kind in the ordshire and Black Country wrought nail trade. Thomas Tinsley married Eliza in 1839; he was thirty and she was ty-five. When her husband died suddenly in 1851 aged forty-two, instead of selling up to concentrate on raising her ly she took over the business in her own name. She was so successful that she had works and warehouses in Sedgley, ley, Wombourne, Oldswinford, Catshill and Bromsgrove, and employed over 200 people. She retired in 1872 and out to a partnership; the Green family, who had helped her run the business after her husband's death, were bers of that partnership. This picture of the work's offices was taken in May 1970 before the century-old appearance e building was altered by the installation of more modern windows. It remains a major company in the area.

Despite attempts by many local historians to save it from demolition, this building fell victim to land clearance in the 1970s. It was the last example of the once-common Black Country warehouse that supplied iron rods and other materials to the numerous outworks in the area and then sold on their products. It had traditional iron window frames with iron columns supporting the floors. At the rear of the building was a quadrangle, on each side of which were a number of forges and workshops. It was owned by the Willetts family. On the external wall there was a carved building stone inscribed 'S. & G.W. 1877 J. Cockin Builder.' The 'S. & G.W.' referred to were Solomon and George Willetts; the builder was probably Mr Cockin of Old Hill. In Kelly's 1904 Directory they were described as 'chain and rivet manufacturers and malleable and cast iron founders'.

ning still taking place within sight (and smell) of advancing industry, *c.* 1900. This dramatic photograph was taken by a
Yelland from Homer Hill. In the centre is a bridge carrying the Stourbridge–Birmingham railway line. On the
me left the roofs of Cradley Forge can be seen and on the skyline to the left are the chimneys of the Earl of Dudley's
d Oak Works, Brierley Hill. On the skyline to the right can be seen Netherton parish church.

A marvellous group photograph of which little is known: what was the event and where was the picture taken? The m
in the centre of the back row (bowler hat, white beard and chain) is Solomon Willetts, who had a warehouse in Lawre
Lane and was a dealer in nails, chains and various oddwork. From scribbled notes around the side of this photogra
dated *c.* 1900 or earlier, we gather that the fourth woman standing from the left is a Mrs Cockin; the man standing at
extreme right is said to be Mr Cooper, the man with the moustache seated extreme right is Mr Palmer, and the M
behind him with the decorative hat is Mrs Carter. Of the four men seated in the centre front row the left two are Geo
and Ted Carter.

A group of women workers from Duckworth's, Station Road, Old Hill, 1950s. In the background is a rare view of
Butterfly Brickworks from which today's 'Butterfly Way' gets its name. Pictured are: (extreme right) Mrs Dor
Underhill (née Bridgwater), while behind her is her sister Joan Bridgwater next to whom are Christine Jackson and Ir
Edge. The only other person identified is Marjorie Hall (extreme left, front row).

CHAPTER SEVEN

TRANSPORT

The GWR was one of the earliest companies to experiment with diesel-engined railcars and here No. W22W is seen by the Cradley Heath goods depot, early 1950s. The car was probably due to run a service from Old Hill along the Windmill End branch line to Dudley – the one-car service known locally as the 'Dudley Dodger'. All the sidings and goods depot were cleared to make way for a new station building, bus station, commuter car park and private housing. Behind the goods depot can be seen the Midland Red bus garage in Forge Lane.

The railway came to Cradley Heath and Old Hill later than most Black Country towns. In 1863 the line was laid from the Oxford–Worcester–Wolverhampton line at Stourbridge Junction to Cradley Heath, and although operated by an independent railway company it eventually became part of the Great Western Railway. The line was later extended to Birmingham.

Until the railway arrived most Cradley Heath firms exported their goods by horse and cart; the New British Iron Company and its predecessor, the Corngreaves Works, were more fortunate for they had a network of narrow gauge lines, one of which connected with the canal between Old Hill and Blackheath.

From Cradley Heath the line has a steeper than average incline on a large embankment to Old Hill; such was the amount of goods traffic that trains were frequently double-headed with a third engine (a banker) pushing from the rear. This was a common sight during both world wars as long trains were marshalled at Cradley Heath.

More than once in the dark days of 1940–2 local townsfolk alongside the line held their breath as some engines literally ran out of steam on the long haul. On occasions enemy bombers were passing overhead en route to bomb Birmingham or Coventry when the firemen had to open the engines' firedoors and frantically shovel in coal to increase steam pressure to restart. Fortunately none of the enemy airmen saw the red shaft of light that pierced the darkness – or if they did they may have thought it was a decoy!

When the embankment was constructed a large mansion, Graingers Hall, had to be demolished. The hall's estate stretched down to the River Stour (Cradley Road) and on to the heathland (Cradley Heath High Street). Where the Cradley Road railway bridge now stands is said to be the site of the hall's small ornamental lake.

At Old Hill Junction a line ran through Halesowen, Romsley and Longbridge to meet the Midland Railway (later LMS). Another branch line ran to Dudley where it met the Oxford–Wolverhampton line, with a further connection to the former London & North Western Railway (later LMS). In their early years both lines were heavily used, none more so than the Longbridge line – which carried hundreds of workers daily to and from the Austin factory during the war years.

Later, with increased competition from road transport, the two branch lines became redundant and were dismantled. The main line, however, is now one of the busiest commuter lines to Birmingham.

This sequence of photographs captures the last days of steam on those two branch lines, and also, literally, the end of the line.

When the diesel railcar wasn't running the service was provided by one of the 'auto trains' – a push-and-pull arrangement; these were a regular sight between Old Hill and Dudley. In this picture of February 1962 the tank engine had 'pushed' the auto-coach to Old Hill. The passenger service was withdrawn, thanks to Dr Beeching's rail 'surgery', on 15 June 1964 – although the line carried goods traffic for some time afterwards, before the line was closed, the track lifted and much of the land given over to factory estates and housing.

The old Cradley Heath station as an ex-GWR pannier tank engine has a run at the incline up to Old Hill, 1962. The station building was built when the Stourbridge–Birmingham (Snow Hill) line opened in 1863. In 1984 the 'up' platform in the background was demolished and a new station erected, together with a bus station, on land formerly occupied by goods sidings and a marshalling yard. The railway signal-box was removed in more recent times and has been rebuilt at the Tyseley Railway Museum, Birmingham.

Cradley Heath station level crossing, little changed since the turn of the century, early 1970s. Since this photograph was taken the gates have been removed and replaced with automatic barriers. The original GWR signal box is on the left, while the building in the centre was originally owned by Rowland Priest, an internationally known firm of chain makers and specialists in the production of block chain for pulley block systems. The upper bay window of the director's office can be seen above the delivery van.

Cradley Heath's original station buildings, dating from April 1863, photographed from the 'down' platform, October 1976. At this time the platforms were staggered. In the rebuilding work in recent years the footbridge has been repositioned and a new 'up' platform built on the site of the sidings, both platforms now being opposite each other. At the same time the line was being built to Birmingham a branch was constructed to serve a local colliery and the ironworks.

Not exactly the 'last train to San Fernando' but certainly the Dudley–Old Hill line was due for closure – even though only a few years before the Old Hill (High Street) Halt platforms (seen here on 24 August 1963) had been rebuilt. The driver, in the front of the auto-coach, wasn't very pleased to see the photographer: he obviously thought he was 'from management'. On 15 June 1964 the line was closed to passenger traffic.

goods train about to leave Old Hill bound for Halesowen, 30 May 1959. The platform in the foreground had been ended with wooden sleepers shortly after war broke out, to accommodate the longer passenger trains that ran a ular service to the Austin factory at Longbridge.

h the Halesowen–Longbridge line facing imminent closure, the Stephenson Locomotive Society chartered a special ewell' steam-hauled special on the line. Here, on 2 November 1963, the train leaves Old Hill. The second set of rails the platform had already been removed. Some freight traffic ran for a time to the Stewarts & Lloyds tube works, ough the line beyond Halesowen had been lifted. Eventually the Old Hill–Halesowen line was also removed.

A s buses began to put in an appearance to offer cheap and quick transport to areas not served by direct rail services, there was a battle royal between competing companies such as Midland Red, Samuel Johnson 'Supreme' of Stourbridge, the Grey Cars of Stourbridge and the Blue Cars of Cradley Heath. The battle was won by Midland Red who, to capture the passenger traffic on a certain route, would put two of their own vehicles to go in front of and behind a competitor's vehicle.

Many of the basic routes of sixty years ago still remain, but with the advent of deregulation and the expansion of residential areas there's not only a variety of coloured buses but a bewildering choice of routes, many of which are much longer and take more time than their predecessors. There were two bus termini in Cradley Heath – one in Graingers Lane and one at the passenger entrance to the railway station. With the clearance of the railway sidings and marshalling yard and the large goods department shed, the land was used to build a bus station for all routes to, from and through Cradley Heath.

Cradley Heath Bus Garage, *c.* 1970. Opened in March 1939, this was the only Midland Red garage to have an air-shelter included in its design; the Second World War broke out six months later. The garage closed in 1971 and l became a pedal cycle factory and warehouse. Many are the tales told of the conductors (when, it is said, a bus was a n personal vehicle) who had their own phrases for certain stops – examples being 'the Kremlin' (Rowley Regis Cou offices), 'the Rest Centre' (the Midlands Electricity Board headquarters at the top of Muckow Hill), and, for the n well-known pubs, 'the Thirst Clinic'.

A 'FEDD'-type double-decker (built in 1933) on the Cradley Heath–Dudley–Wednesbury route waiting at Cradley Heath's old station, September 1951. These vehicles served the Black Country well for twenty-four years before being withdrawn. Sadly none of this type was preserved.

A 'SON'-type single-decker, usually found on the Cradley Heath–Stourbridge and Halesowen routes, outside the Cradley Heath garage, 1950. This type was withdrawn in 1955 but an example has been fully restored and preserved at the Wythall Bus Museum.

A later 'FEDD'-type double-decker arriving at Four Ways, Cradley Heath, from Wednesbury, and stopping out. Bowen-Davies's shop, 1959. Next door was Hinde's opticians, a business that was in the town for many years.

The junction of St Anne's Road and Foxoak Street, with a D5 Dudley–Darby End, Cradley Heath bus, 1968. Fox Street was once a hive of large and small chainshops side by side with terraced houses, but now largely comprises facto and warehouses. Two of the earlier firms based in Foxoak Street, the chainmaking firm of Joseph Woodhouse & Sons and Forward Manufacturing, are no longer in existence. The garage and filling station was originally owned by Regir Clarke Ltd, but was sold in the late 1950s.

charabanc trip assembling outside the Holly Bush Inn, Cradley Heath, *c.* 1918. The Black Country Society's coach and
s expert has identified this vehicle as a Maudslay. The registration FD 1432 indicates it was first registered in Dudley; it
s also been established that it belonged to the firm of Preece, Smith, of Cinder Bank, Netherton. At the extreme right
the picture can be seen the doorway to the Empire Theatre, the site of which is now a public car park.

other mystery picture, except that the building behind looks very much like Holden and Hunt's in Cox's Lane, Old
. But whose 'mini' charabanc was it? Who were the men on board? And where were they going? In particular, the
hors would be delighted to know the identity of the 'toff' with the monocle sitting in the front seat!

A rarely seen photograph of the *Titanic*'s anchor, about to leave Netherton for Belfast. The picture was taken from canal towing path opposite Lloyd's Testing House just after the 16-ton Hall's Patent Stockless anchor had been loaded to a specially strengthened London & North Western Railway cart: note the thickness of the wheels. Although close 1990, the Test House buildings were, when this book was published in late 1998, still in place. On the wharf edge stocked Royal Navy anchor; on the canal are examples of Bantock-owned narrowboats.

This building is reminder of the days when trams clattered their way into Cradley Heath and Old Hill from Dudley an Blackheath.

A former electricity sub-station, it was built by the Midla Electric Power Co. (later to become part of the Midlands Electricity Board) to supply power to the tramway. It was bu to coincide with the opening of the tramway in October 190 Now disused, the substantial building still stands; the proper (including the hairdresser) next door was demolished severa years ago to make room for a factory car park.

CHAPTER EIGHT

SCHOOLS

An etching of the first school at Reddal Hill. It was built in 1790 – many years before Cradley Heath
became big enough to warrant a mention on maps. The school was financed by a charitable trust set up by
George Mackmillan (there's a road named after him in Blackheath), a horn button maker of Rowley Regis,
on land formerly owned by the then Viscount Dudley and Ward. It was replaced in 1876 by the present
building, which later became a community centre in the 1990s.

Corngreaves Infants and Junior School was built in 1848–9 by the New British Iron Company, owned by the Duke Sutherland, for its employees' children's education. In 1896 it was rebuilt to increase its capacity from 275 to children. This is the school's Group III class in 1898–9. One person identified is (second left, top row) John Ball, wh name is mentioned frequently in this book, and who later became a headmaster, a councillor and local magistrate.

Listed in Kelly's Directory of 1896 as Corngreaves Board School in Meredith Street, Reddal Hill, the school w demolished in 1988 after having been disused for some time. This photograph shows the teaching staff in 1920. Back r left to right: Mr Hackett, Mr Richards, Mr John Ball, Mr Brittain, Mr Yates. Front row: Miss Webster, Mr Twigg, Ralph Minty (headmaster), Mrs Hancox.

e final year girls' class at Lomey Town (now Lower High Street) Schools, Cradley Heath, 1927. One person identified Hazel Homer, on the extreme right of the middle row.

esowen Road Junior and Senior Schools, between Old Hill and Netherton, *c.* 1960. They were made of corrugated-sheets fixed to a timber frame. When the school was demolished in 1963 the sheeting was still in good condition ite its age. The sheets were probably made at the nearby Noah Hingley's works, also believed to have provided the ting for two shops built in Cole Street, Darby End. Such unusual construction prompted the nicknames the 'Iron ools' and 'Tin College'.

Wrights Lane Schools, Old Hill, were built in 1898, and in 1998 pupils celebrated the centenary by dressing up in as n[e]
Victorian school costume as possible (below). Between 1900 and 1902 it became a Higher Grade School. Then in 192[5]
became the selective 'Central School' and remained as such until September 1946, when it became Rowley Re[gis]
Grammar School (the headmaster was George Lloyd). It was renamed Temple Meadow School in February 1962, whe[n a]
new purpose-built Grammar School was opened on top of the Rowley Hills at Hawes Lane.

CHAPTER NINE

CHURCHES & CHAPELS

The Clock chapel, Graingers Lane, c. 1885. After the chapel was abandoned, the tower was removed for safety reasons. For several years the semi-circular tablet above the top centre window and the oblong commemorative tablet above the entrance could not be found. Eventually they were discovered serving as doorsteps to two local houses, and were returned to the new church for safe keeping.

Parish churches were established in Cradley Heath and Old Hill in the second half of the nineteenth century. With the rapid expansion of industrial areas following the industrial revolution, Methodism, since described as the workers' religion, grew rapidly. Reports from the time describe the fiery sermons and how ministers and lay preachers would read out the words of each line of the hymns, as very few of the earliest congregations could read or had entered a church before the arrival of Methodism.

With the counter-attraction of television, the mobility of a motor car and other attractions, congregations began to dwindle after the Second World War, with the result that some towns now have one Methodist church where once there were several.

The most well-documented histories of any of the many Methodist churches in the district is that of Graingers Lane Methodist church, Cradley Heath. It was the first Methodist Society to be formed in Cradley Heath and held its first services in a nailmakers' forge in Tibbetts's Gardens (now Northgate) in 1827. As numbers increased two cottages were rented and converted into what a church publication of the time described as 'a spacious meeting-house'. In 1841 the first church was built, and soon became known as the Clock chapel on account of its somewhat ornate (for that area) tower and clock. But in 1895 massive mining subsidence directly under the church resulted in the building being abandoned. In 1906 a new church (standing today) was erected alongside the Sunday schools further up Graingers Lane.

The new Sunday school, *c.* 1895, some ten years before the new church was built. Between the abandonment of Clock chapel and building the new church, the services were held in the school hall. In the Great Depression of the 19 it was used for payment of unemployment benefit. Some 'modernisation' took place in the 1960s but high maintena and heating costs, as well as a lack of use, led to its demolition just as this book goes to press, in late 1998.

architect's drawing shows how much the building leaned
of perpendicular after the subsidence occurred. After the
r and interior balconies had been removed the building
then used for a variety of purposes. The first recorded use
as a carpenters and coffin makers. Then in the late 1920s
came a motor garage. It closed in 1934, but reopened in
ownership of Reginald Clarke — who stayed there until
when he opened larger modern premises in Lower High
t (Lomey Town). It also served as a paint warehouse
il Parkes) and as other business premises before being
olished in a wholesale clearance of all the older properties
raingers Lane. The only building still standing in the
ity is the New Inn, on the extreme left.

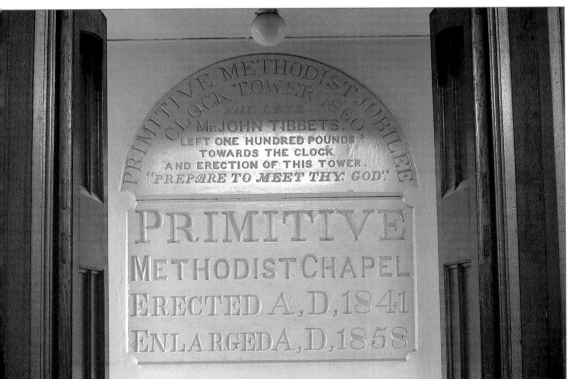

two tablets that were once embedded in the front walls of the old Clock chapel in Graingers Lane. The top tablet
rds the legacy of £100 by John Tibbetts towards the cost of the clock, and the bottom one records the church's
rgement in 1858 — seventeen years after the church was built. They are now preserved in today's church hall.

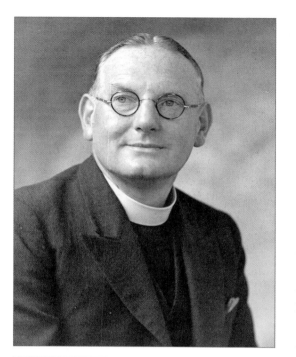

Of the many ministers and clergy in the district one of the
known was the Revd Walter C. Chrimes of Graingers Lane
Apart from his pastoral work and personal interest in the S
of Rest movement, he played a leading role in many of the
town's organisations and their fund-raising activities,
particularly during the war years. He was an official of the
Cradley Heath Choral Society and the Cradley Heath Old
Pensioners Christmas Party Fund, and in many other local
welfare organisations.

The opening of Dudley Wood Methodist church, Dudley Wood Road, 23 October 1907. The earlier 'Mount Z
church on the same site had been wrecked by mining subsidence, as were many other properties in the area. Some ho
remained occupied, albeit leaning at seemingly ridiculous angles, until the 1950s.

These two pictures were taken *c.* 1928 of (above) either the 'Sisters' Class' or the 'Women's Own' at Graingers Lane Methodist Church, Cradley Heath and (below) of the Sidesmen's 'Committee'. Identified in the picture above, front row, left to right: Mrs Lois Woodhouse, Mrs Head, Mrs Samuel Woodhouse, Miss Ruth Tromans, Mrs Henry Woodhouse, Mrs Wilkinson, Mrs Chatwin, -?-, -?-, -?-. Middle row: Mrs Wilfred Woodhouse, -?-, -?-, -?-, Miss Oldacre, -?-, Mrs Clara Ashmore, -?-, -?-, -?-, Mrs Clift, -?-, -?-, Miss Hannah Edmunds, -?-. Back row: -?-, -?-, Mrs Bert Davies, Mrs Head, Mrs Chatwin, -?-, Miss Eliza Williams, Mrs Nellie Scriven, Mrs Cox, -?-, -?-, -?-.

Below, front row, left to right: Harold Totney, Mr Hackett, John Ball, Wilfred Woodhouse, Albert Woodhouse (senior), Rev. J.T. Wilkinson, Joe Poole (senior), Horace Hackett, Mr Horton, Harry Fletcher. Back row: Mr Ball (senior), -?-, Mr Nicklin, Harry Stringer, -?-, Mr Thomas, Mr Poole (junior), Harold Woodhouse, Albert Woodhouse (junior), Walter Guest, Jack Timmington, Will Johnson, Arthur Woodhouse, Horace Head, Harry Raycord, Mr Homer, Joe Pardoe.

Old Hill parish church was built in 1876 at a cost of £15,219, on land provided by the New British Iron Company. This photograph shows building work taking place on the new Staffordshire police station and magistrates' court, c. 1895. Alongside the railings of the church a new road was built, Court Street. This photograph was taken from the bridge carrying the narrow gauge mineral railway from the New British Ironworks at Cradley Heath to the coal mines and canal beyond Old Hill. On the left is part of Zions Hill Methodist church; to the left of the church tower is the Old Hill Board (later Junior Mixed) School; while to the right just visible at the other end of the church are the offices of the former Rowley Regis Board of Guardians (and later the Urban District Council).

Cradley Heath parish church, St Luke's, showing its original appearance, c. 1914. Owing to excessive air pollution the sandstone bricks and the decorative minarets became badly eroded and restoration work was completed in 1928, the minarets being removed. Next door to the church is part of Weston's Dairy with a sign 'New Milk — 3d a quart'. In the late 1920s Mr Weston also ran the Blue Bus Company, but after a long and acrimonious battle with Midland Red for passengers, Midland Red bought his vehicles.

The imposing façade of the Tabernacle Methodist church, High Street, Old Hill, 1970. It was built in 1869 and the Victoria Schools were added in 1897. The church also gave its name to the Tabernacle Amateur Operatic Society, whose productions were held in the Schools. But like many of the older church buildings in the area, the escalating costs of heating and maintenance and dwindling congregations led to a smaller church being built in Lawrence Lane, Old Hill, which also replaced a number of other Methodist churches. The buildings were offered for sale in May 1983 when the new church opened, and in 1986 they were demolished to make way for housing.

St James's Wesleyan Methodist church and its Sunday school at Old Hill Cross was more popularly known as the 'rhubarb chapel', and was opened in 1876. How it came by its nickname is open to debate: one theory is that it was built on the site of rhubarb fields; the other is that at the Harvest Festival services of 100 years ago the gifts were mainly of bundles of rhubarb sticks. In the publicity announcing the closing service on 12 July 1987 after 111 years, it was declared that the organ (valued at £30,000) would be demolished along with the church – so furious was the congregation that their church and Sunday school had to make way for a traffic island.

Trinity Schools in Halesowen Road, Old Hill, were the Sunday schools of the parish church. They were built towards the end of the nineteenth century at a cost of £9,000, and were paid for by Mr G.A.H. Haden-Best of Haden Hall (now Haden Hill Park House). The building had a distinctive red brick façade with Bath stone dressings. At the far end of the building, an extension that jutted out became the home of the first Rowley Regis fire station. Nearest the camera, what was possibly the caretaker's house eventually became a newsagent's and the district office of the *County Express* weekly newspaper. For many years it was owned by Mr and Mrs Horace Sadler, well-known professional ballroom dancing teachers. This picture was taken shortly before demolition in January 1971.

Spring Meadow Particular Baptist church was built in 1841. This photograph was taken in 1971 to record the original frontage before the present brick facing was added. The chapel has its own burial ground at the rear.

A group of Dudley Wood Methodist Sunday school pupils, several of whom became quite well known in the district, late 1940s. Back row, left to right: Jim Billingham, Jim Dunn, Ernest Parkes (later Managing Director of William Stevens Ltd, Brook Lane, Old Hill), Sam Thompson. Middle row: Emily Willetts (later a teacher at Dudley Wood School and the last private owner of what became the preserved Mushroom Green Chainshop), Winnie Smith, Mabel Nicklin, Lucy Bennett (as Councillor Lucy Hingley she became Mayor of Dudley), Cissie Whitehouse, Winnie Ross. Front row: Mary Stevens, Nancy Guest, Hilda Smith, Ruby Priest.

The Methodist churches of the Black Country were famed for their Sunday school anniversaries and this one, held by Christ Church, Cradley Heath, in the Whitley Memorial Schools in 1920 was typical of such happy occasions.

This is thought to be a Sunday School treat at Orchard Road, late 1940s. Bert Morris is handing out the goodies with wife Nancy (facing the camera) helping out. Mrs Morris was the daughter of 'Billy' Biggs, the proprietor of the well known Cradley Heath High Street newsagent and sweet shop.

The 2nd Netherton (Dudley Wood) Girl Guides, based at St John's Church, Dudley Wood, on the banks of the Mousesweet Brook, which marked the Staffordshire and Dudley County Borough boundary. This photograph was taken in about 1945. Back row, left to right: Josephine Cooksey, Sheila Bent, Jean Pearson, Dawn Rowley, Glenys Guest, Pearl Bradley, Janet Price, Margaret Billingham and Janet Cooksey. Middle row: Rita Davies, Edna Carrier, Jean Parkes (now Bridgwater), the Vicar, Rev. Mr Vial, Mrs Vial, Janet Weaver, June Williams and Kathleen Russon. Front row: Edna Smith, Ann Cox, Margaret Cooper, Mary Childs and Maureen Ashman.

CHAPTER TEN

PROCESSIONS, CARNIVALS, PERSONALITIES & SPORT

In the early twentieth century every Sunday school had an annual parade — probably the forerunner to the Sunday school 'treat' when trips were made first by horse brake, then by coach and sometimes train, to the countryside, such as Habberley Valley (near Kidderminster), Kinver and Clent. This Primitive Methodist Sunday school event in Graingers Lane appears to be assembling outside the church. On the right is Harris's general stores. The building on the brow of the hill with an extension on to the pavement later became two shops, one a general grocers, and the other a haberdashery owned by the Totney family for a number of years.

Unlike many towns and districts, the area covered by this book was such that very few 'postcard' views were ever taken. Eighty years ago such a heavily industrialised locality was hardly considered photogenic. Consequently the Industrial Archaeology Group of the Black Country Society is always on the lookout for scenes of local life for its archives whether they be works groups, presentations, church harvest festivals and anniversaries, flower, vegetable and dog shows, parades, carnivals and so forth: in other words, anything that depicted life in the area over the years.

The authors invite readers to contact them via the Society if they have any photographs, drawings, documents or other information which relate to events and organisations in Cradley Heath, Old Hill and district over the past 150 years. With the consent of the owners, such material would be carefully copied, and the originals returned.

If you can help, please write to the authors (Ron Moss and Bob Clarke) via Black Country Society (Industrial Archaeology Group), PO Box 71, Kingswinford, DY6 9YN.

A procession carrying the banner of the Macefields Mission Sunday school makes its way down Halesowen Road, Hill, c. 1918. It is passing the Gate Hangs Well, with the Wesleyan Methodist church in the background on the right. tram line was the route from Old Hill to Blackheath. All the property on the left was demolished in the 1990s. The building to be knocked down was the public house after there had been unsuccessful attempts to reopen it pub/restaurant. The tramway opened on 19 November 1904 and closed on 30 June 1927. It is likely that the Wesl church will be the next building to be demolished.

the postcard says is 'Sunday Parade 1913'. But by whom? The man in the centre appears to be wearing a chain of ce, while further back there is a man holding what could be a ceremonial staff or wand. We can only guess at the anisation but it could be either the local Lodge of the RAOB (Buffaloes) or the Order of Foresters. Both organisations e active in the town at the time. The procession may have been returning from a special service in St Luke's parish rch, seen in the background.

ocession near Four Ways, Cradley Heath, 1913. Where it was from or where it was going is not recorded. It may something to do with the Methodist Christ Church, as it has been suggested the man in the light suit near the head of rocession is Thomas Deeley. In the background is the clothing store of Hammersley's and immediately next door is Round's chainshop. The property was later developed as Round's Furniture Store.

Foxoak Street, Cradley Heath, filled with Christ Church (Methodist) Sunday school children on their way to their annual treat, *c.* 1910. Where they were heading is something of a mystery, but possibly they were going to some of the fields in the Mousesweet Brook area off Cradley Road, Netherton.

Another scene of a Christ Church Sunday school treat, near Four Ways, Cradley Heath, *c.* 1910. The cart at the rear probably belonged to Thomas Bantock's haulage business; he was agent for the Great Western Railway at Cradley Heath goods depot. The leading cart is of a different design and must have belonged to a local company.

A typical Black Country carnival band poses for the photographer in the yard of the Old Engine Inn in Waggon Street, Old Hill, mid-1920s. The poster describes them as the 'Masked Jazz Band – It's Out for Your Money'. Groups like this raised substantial sums of money in aid of local charities and hospitals. Above the wall can be seen the pit mound of the former Black Waggon Colliery.

Dad's Army on parade. Despite the music hall jokes, the Home Guard knew what rifles were for, and the local 'C' Company No. 10 Platoon of the 40th South Staffs Home Guard proved the point when they won the Battalion Rifle Competition in 1944. They posed with their trophy on the steps of the Judge Ware offices, Woods Lane, Cradley Heath.

May 1945, and VE (Victory in Europe) celebration street parties were in full swing nationwide. In Surfeit Hill, Cradley Heath, a children's party was organised by Mr and Mrs Frank Chapman and Mr and Mrs Reg Clarke in the grounds of their home, Greenfield House. Pictured are the parents, among whom are Frank Chapman (seated on the right) and Harold Whitehouse (extreme left). In the centre row on the left are Reg Clarke and Mrs Myra Chapman. On the extreme right of the centre row is Mrs Whitehouse and fourth from right is Mrs Birks. Others pictured include Mrs Bytheway, Mrs Coley, the Misses Coley, Mrs Bradley, Mrs Moy, Mrs Stokes and Mrs Ward. The picture was taken by Mrs Clarke.

scenes of Cradley Heath Carnival procession coming down Spinners' End (later known as Upper High Street), 30. The photographs were taken by Mr Jones from the bedroom window above his shoe shop. Above: a Birch's Best d van has to wait at the entrance of Holly Bush Street for the procession to pass; the left-hand-drive car in the ssion appears to be under tow, while at the extreme top left children perch precariously on a ledge over a shop ow. Below: the procession continues; the man carrying the sign 'Comley's Cradley Carnival Cadets' appears to be ng a 'paper trumpet' band.

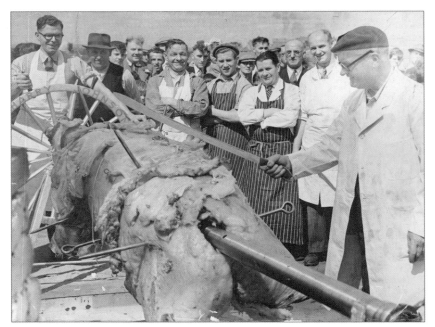

One of the brightest characters in Cradley Heath's leisure time was 'champion ox roaster' Harry Johnson, seen here about to ceremoniously cut the first slice of beef for public auction at a Black Country fête, late 1940s. His son Gilbert is pictured in charge of the wheel that turned the 2½ in diameter tubular spit. Mr Johnson senior was originally an electrician at Noah Hingley's Netherton works; later he founded his own electrical contracting business, which he ran from his home in Cradley Road.

Mr Johnson was always ready to take part in charity work in the town, and he and his son are pictured here on their motor-cycle combination, suitably dressed up, about to join a Cradley Heath Carnival procession in about 1930.

Harry Johnson was a well-known sight around Cradley Heath on his motor-cycle combination. He is seen here out for a ride with his wife Lily and son Gilbert in August 1914.

Seen here on leave during the First World War, John Ball was later to become a well-known figure in the Borough of Rowley Regis. Training as a teacher at Exeter, when war broke out he volunteered and joined the Devonshire Regiment. He was taken prisoner just before Christmas 1917 and on Christmas Day was transferred to a prisoner of war camp on the border of Poland and Russia. On repatriation he resumed his career in teaching and eventually became headmaster of Old Hill Junior School, the old Board School. He was also a Rowley Regis magistrate, and served for a time as councillor on the local borough council.

The Joneses were one of the best-known retail families in Old Hill and Cradley Heath. They founded the well-known shoe shops in Reddal Hill Road and, later, in Halesowen Road, Old Hill, of which the former is still in existence. In this family portrait of about 1917 are the business's founder John (extreme right), and from the left his second son Bert, his wife Phoebe, and the youngest son Howard. At the time this picture was taken the eldest son, John Cooksey-Jones (he added his mother's surname), was serving with distinction in the army.

John Cooksey-Jones joined the army as a Private and served in the Worcestershire and Gloucestershire Regiments. Rising through the ranks, he joined the Royal Fusiliers as a Second Lieutenant. He was a former pupil of King Edward VI School, Stourbridge, and at the end of the war he featured in a booklet produced by the school that listed the war-time exploits of its old boys. It stated that John Cooksey-Jones was Mentioned in Dispatches twice and was three times wounded in action – on 24 June and 9 September 1915, and on 19 June 1916 during the Battle of the Somme. After the war Cooksey-Jones either joined or was transferred to the Indian Army with whom he served with equal distinction, rising to the rank of Brigadier. On leaving the army he returned to his roots and served in the family shoe shop.

While John Cooksey-Jones's military exploits were naturally of great pride to his family, and indeed to his old school and home town, his son Richard Stanton-Jones (like his father he added his mother's maiden name) gained international fame as an aeronautical designer and, some say, was the driving force behind Britain's one-time superiority in design and construction of hovercraft. He is pictured here in readiness for a local carnival, *c.* 1930.

Roughly twenty-five years after the family portrait of about 1917, Howard Jones was also in uniform – serving with the local Home Guard during the Second World War.

Richard Stanton-Jones, like his father, went to King Edward VI School, Stourbridge. He then gained entrance to King's College, Cambridge, where this photograph was taken. From university he joined the Cranfield College of Aeronautics and in the 1950s his brilliant engineering mind led him to become chief designer for Saunders-Roe at their Isle of Wight headquarters, where he worked on the Black Knight and other British rockets and missiles. He was also engaged on design work for supersonic fighter aircraft.

When Saunders-Roe became part of the British Hovercraft Corporation, Stanton-Jones worked on eight types of experimental hovercraft. Rising to managing director, he was solely responsible for the trail-blazing 150-ton SRN4 hovercraft – though strangely he never appears to have been given the public recognition he so richly deserved.

Thanks in no small measure to his work, the company received the Queen's Award to Industry for Hovercraft Technical Innovation in 1966. His personal brilliance and design work was recognised in the USA, and in 1968 he received the American Sperry award for Leadership and Engineering Skill. Stanton-Jones was also elected a Fellow of the British Inter-Planetary Society and a Member of the Institution of Naval Architects. Sadly he died in 1990 at the comparatively early age of sixty-four.

One of the longest-serving church organists in the district was William H. Smith. He was organist at Graingers Lane Methodist church, Cradley Heath, for forty-five years; he was also closely associated with many major musical events and organisations in the district, including Cradley Heath Choral Society, whose concerts for many years were held on the stage of the Majestic Cinema (now a bingo hall). Guest artistes included Kathleen Ferrier and Owen Brannigan.

Spinners End, Cradley Heath, was said to have gained its name from the arrival during the last century of weavers from the continent. Later it became officially known as Upper High Street and it was there that the former Ruth Stone, later Mrs Turnhill, was a milliner for many years. She and her husband were also proprietors of a newsagent's business in Corngreaves Road, Cradley Heath.

The real thing: a true Black Country pub. The Old Cross Guns in Cradley Road, Cradley Heath, was the sportsm
pub. Sadly the arrival of so-called smart pubs outside the town, with car parking, and the de-population of the centre
Cradley Heath during house clearance schemes, led to its eventual closure. For years, if anyone wanted to know anyth
about pigeon racing, whippet and dog racing, football, and above all Staffordshire Bull Terriers, then the Old Cross G
was the place to visit. The pub manager (second from right) is Joe Mallen and the picture is thought to have been ta
between 1938 and 1940. Mr Mallen had also been engaged in the iron ring and shackle making trade. With him at the
are, left to right, Ted Rock, Percy Bishop, Freddy Guy and Billy Cartwright.

Before Mr Mallen's arrival, the Old Cross Guns had a dubious if not fearsome reputation. A local historian o
claimed that the pub had been suspected of having cockfighting in its cellars and that some of the locals had not b
averse to putting rats in a barrel and taking bets on how long it would take a terrier (usually a Staffordshire Bull Terr
to kill them.

The authors are grateful to Mrs Ann Wilson of Stratford-upon-Avon for some of the background to the Old C
Guns and her father, Arthur Fellows, who identified the people in the pub.

She also tells of Mrs Mallen's generosity to local families to whom she gave food during the General Strike. N
Wilson recalls Mrs Mallen giving her grandmother one (old) penny to pay her for her daughter's christening. T
example of Black Country generosity has never been mentioned before. Mrs Wilson also said she used to live in Sur
Hill, Cradley Heath.

Joe Mallen. Under his right arm he holds a fighting cock, while with his left he holds a Staffordshire Bull Terrier – a breed that he fought long and hard to be accepted nationally as a breed in its own right . . . a battle he won.

Mr Mallen took great pride in the eventual acceptamce by the Kennel Club of the Staffordshire Bull Terrier as a breed in its own right. This picture was taken at one of the early appearances of the breed at Blackpool Dog Show, 23–24 June 1937. An interesting message (top right) asks owners to make arrangements for the collection of their dogs for the return journey; at that time dogs were not allowed to travel in trains with their owners, but had to travel in a special cage in either the goods or guards van.

This all-ladies' coach trip (except for the driver) was an outing 'from Cradley to Matlock': what the party was and where the folk came from is not recorded. It may have been in Cradley Heath, for even today people will refer to 'Cradley' when they mean Cradley Heath. That said, it would have taken them a fair time to reach Matlock, for the coach has a notice underneath the front passenger door: 'Speed 12mph'. The vehicle's front tyres are pneumatic while the rear wheels have solid tyres. Some ride . . . !

A ladies' parade along Halesowen Road, Old Hill, near the junction with Trinity Street, c. 1920. What the event was is not recorded, but it may have been a parade from the nearby parish church to Trinity Schools.

assembly hall of the 'Iron School', Halesowen Road, Netherton, *c.* 1927. Who is the master (or is it the headmaster) solated splendour? Note the wooden cladding of the walls and roof, which were made of corrugated-iron sheeting.

party of girls being 'bussed' to cookery (or home economic) classes from Cradley Heath County Secondary School, itehall Road, *c.* 1966.

When some houses in Station Road, Old Hill, were being cleared prior to demolition, members of the Black Country Society were invited to search the buildings for any memorabilia. Among the items found were these two delightful and well-preserved pictures dating from Victorian times. But who were the

people? Were they Old Hill people or had they moved from elsewhere? Answers would be gratefully received by the Society.

Old habits and traditions die hard. Even into the 1950s there were some traders engaged in home deliveries who relied on the horse-drawn cart or van. Above: a horse-drawn greengrocer's cart in Dalvine Road, Dudley Wood, 1950. Below: Isaiah Collins's baker's cart (with pneumatic tyres!) in Dalvine Road, 1951. Collins's Bakery stood at the corner of Newton Lane and Foxoak Street, Cradley Heath, opposite the Salvation Army citadel.

earlier pages we have featured some of the Cradley Heath Home Guard members with rifle competition trophies they
won. This photograph is thought to be the formal (and final) photograph of the whole Battalion (40th South Staffs)
ore they were 'stood down' as the Second World War drew to a close. They are pictured outside Ernest Stevens's
lgeware works in Woods Lane, Cradley Heath, in 1944. Ernest Stevens is believed to be seated in the centre, but sadly
re is no identification of any other men. Close inspection shows that many, particularly the NCOs, are wearing
npaign ribbons, presumably of the First World War.

ousehold name around Cradley Heath and Old Hill
he late 1940s and '50s was that of the Valeting
vice, a prosperous laundry and dry cleaning
npany. Here two of the young ladies employed there
e in the car park: on the left is Sylvia Griffiths, while
Cox is on the right.

The works and office staff of Stevens Brothers, Foxoak Street, Cradley Heath, holloware manufacturers, *c.* 1924. Unfortunately there was no other information with this photograph; it may have marked some event within the company.

Corngreaves Boys' School football team, 1925/6. They must have been a force to be reckoned with judging from this photograph of them with an enormous shield and three cups: unfortunately there is no record of what competitions they won. Back row, left to right: Mr F. Sidaway and Mr J. Ball (teachers), P. Cutler, L. John, A. Allen, Mr P.W. Richards (headmaster). Middle row: J. Patrick, A. Cutler, W. Round (vice-captain), F. Parkes (captain), H. Williams, J. Lewis. Front row: S. Garratt, L. Dunn, T. Pearson, W. Vernon.

A well-known amateur boxer in the early part of the century was Henry Attwood, who in professional life was a butcher in the former High Street, Cradley. This later became a beer house, which developed into the White Horse Inn.

Cradley Heath Football Club were Birmingham League Champions in 1926/7. Team members were as follows: seated white shirts, left to right: Langford, Gibbons, Albert Jones, Bridges, H. Johnson, D. Boxley, Morgan. Front row: Ev S. Taylor, Lowe. Standing in short sleeves is Mr Woodhouse (trainer/manager?). The remainder are thought to be officials and reserve players.

Dudley Wood Vics (from the Victoria Inn, Dudley Wood Road) who won the Wolverhampton & Dudley Brewe Challenge Cup in 1911/12. Behind them is a wall built of lumps of slag from a blast furnace; a chain shop is seen in background. The team's pitch was redeveloped shortly after the Second World War for dog racing and speedway.

...bers of Harcourt Tennis Club, Old Hill, the forerunner of Old Hill Tennis Club, late 1920s. When their courts were ...n over along with other land by Rowley Regis Council to create the Harcourt Road housing estate, the club built new ...ts in Barrs Road adjoining the Old Hill Cricket Club ground. The only person identified is John Ball, extreme left, ... row. On top of the hill at the rear of the courts stood Harcourt House, later to become a private school. This has ...d in the past three years and its grounds have been redeveloped for private housing.

...lley Heath St Luke's Football Team, 1933/4. Back row, left to right: Jim Lane, Walter Hackett, Bert Parsons, Jack ...kes, Fred Cox, -?-, Mr Edwards (churchwarden). Middle row: Piper, the Rev. Gwynffor John (uncle of Mr Griffiths, ...ller, of High Street (Cradley Heath), Arthur Foulkes, Alf Parsons. -?-, the Rev. Mr Thirwell, Ivor Price (Sunday ...ol superintendent). Front row: Sydney Jones, Ted Wakeley, Jack Price, Piper, Pugh.

One of the most popular sports in the Black Country for over a century has been pigeon racing. At one time there v
hardly a street in Old Hill and Cradley Heath that didn't have at least one pigeon loft. Birds were sent, first by train a
now by road, hundreds of miles to be released; at the time the birds were due to return to their lofts men would
anxiously scanning the sky. This scene of one man, his pigeons and the loft would have been much the same 100 years a
as it was when the photograph was taken in 1982.

Whippet racing was a favourite sport in the Black Country at one time. It enjoyed something of a revival locally in the
1960s and early 1970s. This photograph was taken at a race meeting at the Belle Vale end of Haden Hill Park on Sur
morning, 12 July 1970.

tice time at Cradley Heath Speedway, Dudley Wood, early 1960. At this time there were no flashy leathers – just
ured helmets and team waistcoats. Speedway racing started in Dudley Wood in 1947–8 when several riders won
nal honours; names from that period include the Beaumont brothers, Alan Hunt and Phil Malpass. After a short
k it resumed again, only to come to an abrupt halt when the owners of the stadium put the land up for sale.
rlooking the ground, the former pit mound was known as Scotsman's Hill (see above), because people could have a
s-eye view of the racing without paying a penny!

ACKNOWLEDGEMENTS

The authors gratefully acknowledge the assistance of the following in loaning photographs and providing invaluable information:

Joseph Billingham, Clive Bowen-Davies, David Bridgwater, Jean Bridgwater, Norman Bridgwater, Yvonne Brookes, Peter Glews, Elsie May Griffiths (née Johnson), Ron Griffiths, Colin Grinnell, Keith Hodgkins, Leonora Johnson, Mr Jacquiss, Alan Potter, Robert Priest, Alan T. Smith, Anne Smith, Arthur Smith, Doreen Underhill, John Wallin, David Whyley, Ann Wilson, Samuel Woodhouse and Staffordshire Arts and Museum Service, Shugborough.

The authors also wish to pay tribute to the local photographers who have captured scenes of the district over the past 100 years, among whom were Bassano, Beech, Cockin, Everit and Yelland.